Careers
With Young Children:
Making Your Decision

Careers
With Young Children:
Making Your Decision

by

Judith W. Seaver
Early Childhood Consultant
Washington, D.C.

Carol A. Cartwright
The Pennsylvania State University
University Park, Pennsylvania

Cecelia B. Ward
Child Development Council of Centre County
Bellefonte, Pennsylvania

C. Annette Heasley
Executive Secretary
Pennsylvania Consortium for Children
and
Early Childhood Consultant
Columbus, Pennsylvania

National Association for the Education of Young Children
Washington, D.C.

This project was supported by a Membership Action Grant from the National Association for the Education of Young Children. We acknowledge and appreciate NAEYC's support. The content and views presented reflect the work of this Membership Action Group and do not necessarily represent the position of the National Association for the Education of Young Children.

Cover and text photographs by Richard A. LeFande, except for photograph on p. 17 by Marilyn Lamb.

Cover design by Caroline Taylor.

The Decision Survey (pp. 83-87) and the Decision Survey Rating Sheet (pp. 89-90) may be freely reproduced with appropriate credit to the authors.

Library of Congress Catalog Card Number: 78-71950
ISBN Catalog Number: 0-912674-64-4

Printed in the United States of America.

Contents

Foreword

Each of us, consciously or unconsciously, chooses the directions our lives will take. If one of your major interests is the education and well-being of children, you have probably thought about a career that will in some way affect children or their families. This book is designed to help you find out more about what type of job in this field might be best for you.

Whether you are a teenager beginning to plan for your future, a college student ready to select a major, an adult making a career change, or someone looking for new challenges, this book can help you evaluate your skills and interests for a career with children or families.

You will find these sections of the book especially valuable:

- **Decision Survey**—you will be guided in Part B to list and evaluate information about yourself that is pertinent to careers with children or families.

- **Career Patterns**—you will meet several men and women engaged in careers they enjoy and explore with them their skills and backgrounds that led them to their career choice.

- **Resources**—ideas on where to go to learn more about specific occupations.

Choosing a career is one of the major decisions of your life. Even if this book helps you find you are not well-suited to work with children and families, it should be valuable to you as you learn more about yourself.

Jan McClurg
Director of Publications
NAEYC
January 1979

A.

Getting to know your career interests

1

Before you begin

When I grow up, I want to be
A mommy, a daddy, a sailor at sea
Or maybe a builder, or maybe a teacher
Or maybe someone who sits under a
tree.

When I grow up, I want to be
A soldier, a lawyer, a keeper of bees
Or maybe a doctor, or maybe a banker
Or maybe I'll just stay me.

The rhymes of childhood often capture some of life's important concerns. One of these concerns is choosing an occupation. As adults, we must make a commitment to a career to be considered productive, yet the choice of our career must be consistent with personal interests and available job opportunities.

This book presents comprehensive career information to guide those interested in pursuing careers involving young children or their families. You may be starting to think of a career with young children for the first time, you may be thinking of switching settings, or you may be thinking of acquiring extended or advanced training in a specialty area. In any of these circumstances, you will find this book helpful.

Your route to a personally appropriate choice and the acquisition of the training and experience necessary to make you employable need not be haphazard. The growth required, both personally and professionally, to translate budding skills and interests into mature, practiced skills and job competence for a professional career with young children is indeed great. You can do a considerable amount of work to plan ahead for training and experience that will result in a career pattern which is personally and professionally satisfying and stimulating. The decision to work with young children and the selection of a particular career pattern must be a deliberate, systematic effort that is based on a realistic appraisal of personal values and skills and accurate information regarding the job and career options available.

What is early childhood?

The period generally called *early childhood* is the age range from infancy through about age eight or nine. According to most developmental psychologists, early childhood is a period in the development of the individual when change is great and growth is swift. The young child rapidly acquires language, problem solving, and socialization skills. The young child also refines these skills and acquires a sense of self that will remain for life.

Regardless of occupational title or professional role, those at work with children and families come to their jobs with a set of beliefs and attitudes, in addition to their job skills, about how human beings grow and develop. Let's briefly examine three perspectives on development currently being used by early childhood professionals as a basis for planning and implementing services and programs for children and families.

One view of development can be labeled the **behaviorist** perspective. Behaviorists see development as an accumulation of learning that occurs when behaviors are systematically rewarded. The child is seen as a "responder" to the environment. This view of development has greatly influenced early childhood programs and services and suggests that anyone can make progress if the appropriate situations are provided in the environment.

Another perspective on development can be labeled **cognitive-interactionist.** Those who hold this view are primarily concerned with the cognitive development of the child. People who hold this perspective see a need to allow the child to accumulate meaningful experiences and then follow through by providing activities that challenge and stretch the child to new levels of thinking. The cognitive-interactionists are most concerned about the processes of learning. Individuals who believe in the cognitive-interactionist view of development are optimistic about programming for young children because they see the objectives of the programs as aimed at helping children acquire thinking processes.

Yet another different perspective on development emphasizes the **maturationist** or **whole child** approach to development. Development is seen as the unfolding, or maturation, of those psychological and physiological elements within the individual at birth. Individuals initiate their own activities because it is assumed they will naturally choose those activities that are most appropriate for their current level of development. The maturationists are more likely than any other group to see early childhood programs and services as a basic human right of every individual.

Early childhood has become a multidisciplinary field as a result of the interest in young children and the expansion of services occurring in the past ten to fifteen years. The different approaches to programming that are an outgrowth of different perspectives on human development contribute to the diversity of roles and responsibilities available to those who are planning a career with young children.

How this book can help you

Traditional job labels such as *teacher* no longer adequately describe the range of career patterns now possible for those who wish to work with young children. Widespread recognition of the importance of early childhood has expanded the number and kinds of settings in which professionals work with young children. For example, professionals who are concerned about young children and families can now be found in such diverse settings as legislatures, hospitals, day care centers, agricultural extension services, public relations firms, courts, churches, government offices, television/radio, newspapers, and department stores.

Accompanying the increase in diversity of settings in which young children are found has been a growing interest in the adequate preparation of professionals. Increasingly, more specialized education and skills are being required. In some circumstances, this training is needed in order to enter a job or a career with young children; in other situations, those already at work are seeing a need for improving their skills and are voluntarily seeking training.

A career with young children implies a long-term commitment directed toward the acquisition of skills and training. This book contains a Decision Survey to guide you in exploring the best fit between your personal characteristics and potential careers in the field. This Decision Survey is organized around three questions that will be explored further in "Surveying your interests in careers with or for young children" (p. 4):

The remainder of the book contains descriptions of various jobs within five different career patterns. This information was obtained through observation and interviews with hundreds of people in careers involving young children and families. Supplemental information on many jobs was gathered from published career information sources.

The Decision Survey provides space for you to write in your own feelings, interests, and skills. There are no right or wrong answers, but this Survey should help you organize your attributes and values as they relate to your possible career with or for young children.

Step 1: Why do you want to work with or for young children?
You will be guided in exploring your feelings about and interest in young children. What aspects of their welfare are of most concern to you? Information in each of the career descriptions will help you to identify appropriate careers.

Step 2: What skills and abilities do you have?
You will be given opportunities to describe and evaluate your personal qualifications.

Step 3: What degree of involvement with children is best for you?
Information describing various jobs can be used to compare and match yourself with different career alternatives.

Surveying your interests in careers with or for young children

Locating oneself vocationally in the future, however defined, must be predicated upon coming to terms with one's values and life purposes, with one's personal characteristics and orientation toward or away from others—in short, those things about the self that can serve as reference points for sorting and evaluating alternatives made available by society. In one sense, nothing is more personal than choosing the way to spend one's life. (Herr and Cramer 1972, p. 3)

The three questions in this chapter will help you look at your thinking about careers with young children or their families. Your active participation is essential to produce personally meaningful results. Perhaps some questions you respond to will be new and cause you to think about careers involving young children in ways you have not done before. Be honest and complete in writing your responses—the more information you use to help make your career decision, the more comfortable and satisfied you will be with that decision.

Reference

Herr, E. L., and Cramer, S. H. Vocational Guidance and Career Development in the Schools: Toward a Systems Approach. Boston: Houghton Mifflin, 1972.

Three Major Questions

Step One: Why do you want to work with or for young children?

_____

_____

_____

_____

_____

_____

Step Two: What are your skills and abilities?

_____

_____

_____

_____

_____

Step Three: What degree of involvement with children is best for you? What job(s) do you see yourself doing?

_____

_____

_____

_____

_____

_____

What responses might indicate why you should pursue a career working with or for young children?

Step One: Why do you want to work with or for young children?

Adults who pursue careers involving young children and families are characterized by a special sense of concern for children. This professional concern is evidenced by a sense of deliberateness and formality expressed in the adult's perception of the value of *all* children to society and a sense of commitment to early childhood as a special developmental period in the lifespan.

Value and commitment. Another way to describe this special, professional sense of concern for young children is to consider the personal values and feelings of commitment this concern reflects. (Values are those things that you consider to be important and meaningful. Commitment is the sense of obligation and responsibility you feel for something.) You may want to make lists of things you value and things to which you are committed, and then rank the items in each list in order of priority. How high would you rank children?

Those who choose careers involving young children and their families generally rank two ideas very highly:

The early years of childhood are valued as an extremely important foundation for later life and learning; *and*

A high degree of commitment is expressed to personal, active participation in shaping individual and group experiences for children.

You may phrase your values and commitments somewhat differently and still indicate a similar high level of concern for children. The implications are that young children are particularly valued by you and that you are committed to actively shaping the course of young children's experiences in some way.

Interest. Interest in young children can take many forms.
Do you like to be with young children?
Do you like to work with families who have young children?
Do you like to share your knowledge about young children with others?
Do you like to be involved with ideas and materials related to young children?

If you answered yes to any of these questions, you probably have a positive interest in young children. Professional interest in young children is often expressed as:

A genuine liking for young children, *and*

A recognition of a personal sense of challenge and stimulation derived from fostering or studying the development of children.

Some adults are challenged by working directly with children in educational settings; others may be interested in working with families in social service agencies; still others may prefer to design children's toys, write children's books, lobby for children's causes, or teach other adults about child care.

Relationships. The associations with others at work often affect the quality and satisfaction we derive from our work. In considering career choices, it is important to understand your personal preferences and skills in developing and maintaining interpersonal relationships.

The ability to develop and maintain relationships with young children is required for any career involving children or any work with adults in preparation to serve children. Relationships with young children almost always involve physical contact and an easy expression of feelings and ideas, both verbally and nonverbally. Baby talk is not advocated; but an ability to use clear language is. The development of language is one of the great landmarks of early childhood growth, and adults who work with young children often single out this aspect of development as an area for particular emphasis.

Children are always part of a family. Adults who work in careers involving young children will always experience some form of contact with the children's families. This necessarily means that some degree of skill in communicating with other adults will be required for all who choose to work with young children. Communication between concerned adults about a particular child will require skill in rapport-building, selection of relevant information, and the ability to explain complex ideas without being condescending. Communication with other

professionals will require a command of literature and information, as well as a high degree of skill in written, oral, formal, and informal communication.

People contemplating careers involving young children must consider two items about relationships that will be part of their daily activities:

The kind of contact preferred with others, *and*

The communication skills with children and adults.

Careers with young children are not solitary, isolated activities, with a few exceptions such as writing children's books. Relationships will be established with the children, with their families, with other professionals, and with the general public.

Time. Children's natural development takes time. Different children will develop at different rates, often unevenly in areas such as physical, social, intellectual, and social-emotional development. Change related to growth and development occurs slowly and often is barely noticeable from day to day or even from week to week.

One of the most exciting aspects of careers involving young children is the opportunity to participate in and guide developmental change. But this is frequently also one of the most frustrating aspects of the same career. Those who work with young children must be particularly observant of small details and changes, as such things signal that developmental change is probably occurring. Working with young children calls for a tolerance and appreciation of small accomplishments and the ability to see how small bits fit into the larger scheme of development (see pp. 2-3).

Those who are anticipating careers involving young children must carefully consider two ideas in relation to the time frame of developmental change:

Efforts directed at producing developmental change and growth in young children do not always yield immediate, visible, or large results; *and*
Initiative and optimism are required to continue working productively over a period of time.

Children are unique beings, and development is affected by many variables. Adults who work directly with young children will be most sensitive to the delayed time frame of feedback for their efforts. Those who work with families will be sensitive to the wide range of conditions that affect change and developmental progress. Those who work with other professionals will constantly consider the many factors that directly and indirectly affect the conditions and settings in which young children experience their daily life.

Authority. How an individual responds to authority and supervision and how effectively an individual can exercise authority are important considerations for any career. Adults working with children will generally be working together in some kind of team. Nurses, social workers, and teachers, for example, are all part of larger teams of professionals whose efforts are jointly directed at providing programs and services for young children.

Two aspects of authority are particularly relevant for careers involving young children: responsibility and accountability. *Responsibility* refers to the extent to which you feel comfortable and are competent enough to take charge. *Accountability* refers to the extent to which you can justify and explain your actions to others.

Responsibility and accountability may seem to be forms of authority that are unrelated to the question of caring for children. However, no career involving young children is exempt from the acceptance and exercise of both of these forms of authority. Adults considering careers involving young children must weigh their own feelings relative to the degree of authority with which they are personally comfortable:

The extent of responsibility they can competently handle, *and*

The acceptance of accountability for their own actions.

All people who perform jobs must be responsible and accountable for their actions in those jobs; however, the general public is voicing increased concern for the well-being of children. Those involved in careers with young children can expect closer scrutiny of their job performances than can workers in many other careers.

Image. Self-image and the image you present to others are not sufficient reasons alone to choose or to exclude certain career options. However, how you view yourself in a job is likely to relate closely to the satisfaction you derive from the job and your stability in that career. How others view you will directly affect your self-image as a career person.

The biggest component of self-image derived from job-related activities is the feeling you have about the worth and satisfaction of the job activities you perform. Careers involving young children can require numerous different kinds of tasks, all of which relate to caring for children. Caring can include expressions of concern ranging from those of a nurse at a child's sickbed to those of a consumer expert testifying before a senate subcommittee on the safety of child restraint devices for automobiles.

The image we present to others is more difficult to pinpoint. Many feel that those who work with young children do so because it is easy and because it does not require much thought and work. Nothing could be farther from the truth, as work with young children is both physically exhausting and intellectually demanding. However, you will at some point in your career life have to confront and defend opinions that seem to be negative. If you are confident in your choice of career and understand and can articulate why your career suits you, such an explanation will not be difficult to give.

Those considering careers involving young children should examine their feelings about image:

If they like to think of themselves caring for or about children, *and*

How they can improve the opinions of others about careers involving young children.

Summary of Key Characteristics of Professional Concern for Children

Step One: Why do you want to work with or for young children?

Value	young children and early childhood as an important period of life
Commitment	to an active role in shaping experiences for many young children
Interest	a liking for young children; a feeling of challenge from involvement in children's development
Relationships	frequent contact with children and adults; established and maintained by various communication skills
Time	developmental change is often not quickly visible; self-initiative is required to function productively
Authority	acceptance of responsibility for one's actions; acceptance of accountability for one's actions
Image	like to think of caring for or about children; how they can improve the opinions of others about careers involving young children

At this point, you may wish to complete Step One of the Decision Survey (p. 83) which further explores your interest and reasons for wanting to work with or for young children. If you choose, you may postpone completing the Decision Survey until you have read the discussion of the remaining two questions.

Step Two: What are your skills and abilities?

Satisfaction and success in your career depend immeasurably on your skills and abilities. What you can do, what you can reasonably learn to do, and what you are reasonably skillful at doing are all important considerations in choosing a career. The descriptions and explanations given in this section will be focused on situations specific to skills and abilities that relate to careers involving young children.

Skill implies some degree of measured competence and performance. There are obviously many levels of skill, but the standard most meaningful in the working world is, "Are you good enough for someone to pay you for exercising your skills?" There are two ways of documenting your skills: One is education; the other is experience. Both education and experience indicate to a prospective employer that you have acquired and demonstrated job-related skills.

Education. For most jobs in our society, a high school diploma is considered to be desirable. Generally a high school diploma indicates that the graduate has basic mathematics, communication, writing, and reading skills. Increasing levels of education are typically associated with specialization and refinement of basic skills. Where a high school graduate may have taken one or two home economics courses in child care, the holder of an associate degree will have taken several courses and participated in some related field experiences.

Some careers involving young children require training and/or certification that can be earned concurrently with a bachelor's degree. Teachers often earn degrees and qualify for teaching certificates simultaneously. Nurses may or may not train in a degree-granting program; but all must pass board examinations for certification. Doctors and lawyers must pass similar licensing examinations that are independent of the degree they earned. The Child Development Associate (CDA) program leads to a certificate of competence that combines education and experience in documenting the skills of individuals.

Many careers require one educational level for entry and then as one gains experience, considerable encouragement, and sometimes pressure, is generated for the individual to upgrade educational skills. People who have earned master's and doctor's degrees typically did so after some initial experiences in jobs that required less formal education. Thus, as in many professions, the route to promotion and transfer of skills between related areas is often tied to the increasing educational progress of an individual.

You can reasonably expect to complete educational levels for which you are academically prepared and capable and which you can finance. College degrees cost money for tuition and room and board. Graduate degrees also require financial outlay as well as a few years of intensive study, which often means leaving a job to devote full time to study. Such a break in employment is not always financially feasible, and such intensive additional training is not always necessary. Conferences, workshops, and books are some of the many ways individuals seek to broaden their knowledge.

Experience. Experience may be paid work or volunteer work in which someone supervises you and is willing to report the nature, extent, and quality of your work.

On the Decision Survey (p. 83) you will describe the experiences you have had related to careers with young children. Describe first the experiences you have had working directly with young children. Next, think about experiences you have had working with the families of young children. Many careers with young children require supervisory skills and experience in organizing events and people. Public speaking, training others to perform tasks, and dealing with the general public are important components of many careers involving young children.

Abilities. Abilities refer to a generalized set of behaviors that you have probably demonstrated in a number of different settings. For example, you may have listed under experience on the Decision Survey that you worked as an aide in a Saturday gymnastics class for preschoolers. Perhaps you also listed that you babysat for a family at the beach one summer. However, these two experiences do not convey fully the extent of your abilities in dealing with young children. In order to describe these abilities, you will have to think of all the times you interacted with children and then list such things as:

You find it easy to talk with children and help them talk about things.

You can plan for and manage a group of small children doing physical activities.

You are sensitive to and skillful in handling young children's feelings.

You can probably think of many other statements that will describe your particular abilities with young children.

You will describe several other kinds of abilities which can relate to various careers with young children and families on the Decision Survey (p. 83). The abilities you have demonstrated in professional and social experiences with adults may include the ability to listen to others, to explain, to interpret, to observe others in action, to support others in pursuit of their goals, to interact easily with adults of many ages, or that you are comfortable with others and converse easily.

Your abilities with groups and organizations are also important. Consider such things as the delegation of responsibility; your supervision of others; your ability to work in cooperative relationships; your ability to share responsibility; and your ability to exercise leadership.

The last question in Step Two relates to abilities that you evidence across situations but that are not related to specific jobs or experiences. Think for a moment about the abilities you have which indicate you are a self-starter: that you can plan, execute, and assess events without continuous supervision and support. *Initiative* is especially important in careers involving young children. Children are unique and hence unpredictable; situations will always arise in which decisions have to be made on the spot or plans changed because of children's unexpected responses. In careers that do not require direct work with young children, many job tasks will be of long duration requiring the individual to plan and work toward a distant goal.

Step Two: What are your skills and abilities?

Education...............formal training that can be documented through a transcript

Experience.............supervised work that someone will reference as to the nature, extent, and quality of your work

Abilities and Initiative .... with Children Adults Groups and Organizations ....generalized behaviors that have been demonstrated in a number of different settings

You may want to complete the second part of the Decision Survey (p. 83) now, or you may wait until the end of the section.

Step Three: What degree of involvement with children is best for you?

Careers in many areas of the field require similar kinds of contact or involvement with young children and their families. Early childhood is also a multidisciplinary field (health, sociology, education, welfare, psychology, recreation, home economics, etc.). Overlap with professionals is common for anyone working with young children and their families. Consequently, career alternatives can be clustered according to the amount of direct contact with young children that each cluster involves. Jobs within a cluster are considered to be similar in contact requirements, although each career within a cluster may differ markedly in many other aspects. Figure 1 illustrates the close relationship of the five career pattern clusters to each other.

Summary

Further details about the five career patterns outlined in Figure 1 are included in the remainder of this book. Based on your current understanding of possible career options, however, **please complete the entire Decision Survey (p. 83–87) before proceeding.**

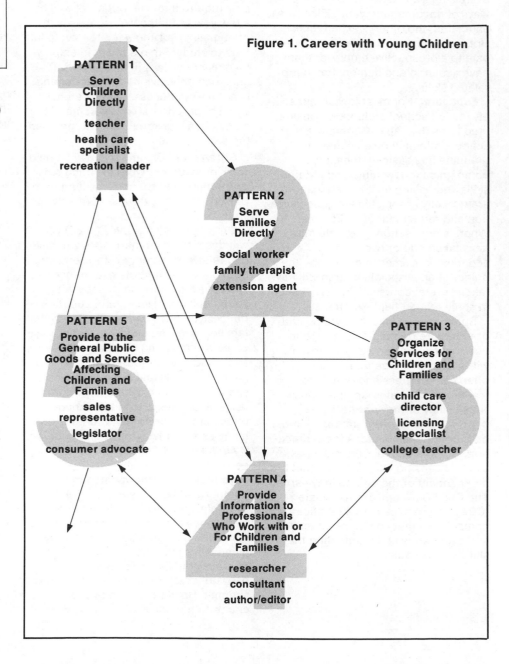

Figure 1. Careers with Young Children

PATTERN 1
Serve Children Directly
teacher
health care specialist
recreation leader

PATTERN 2
Serve Families Directly
social worker
family therapist
extension agent

PATTERN 3
Organize Services for Children and Families
child care director
licensing specialist
college teacher

PATTERN 4
Provide Information to Professionals Who Work with or For Children and Families
researcher
consultant
author/editor

PATTERN 5
Provide to the General Public Goods and Services Affecting Children and Families
sales representative
legislator
consumer advocate

B.

Exploring careers with or for young children

Career Pattern One

Serve Children Directly

Be sure to complete the Decision Survey (pp. 83-87) before continuing.

The greatest degree of involvement with children is evidenced in the careers in pattern one. These include a wide range of professional areas including health, education, psychology, recreation, social service, or home economics. Regardless of the particular content emphasis of an individual's training, that content will be applied in working directly with young children.

Careers in pattern one also vary according to the amount of professional training and the degree of responsibility the individual exercises in planning services for young children. These include individuals who work directly with young children as aides, assistant teachers, assistant group leaders, housekeepers, family day care mothers, and other positions that often do not require extensive professional preparation. Higher levels of professional preparation and responsibility for children's services are required for careers as pediatric nurses; nursery school, child care, or Head Start teachers; school nurses; and primary grade teachers. Considerably more specialized professional training is required for pediatricians, dietitians, speech therapists, physical therapists, and school psychologists.

Individuals in career pattern one have contact with the families of young children and frequently use professional support services of trained specialists in other career patterns. A strong liking for young children that leads to interacting easily and competently with young children is an absolute prerequisite for careers in this pattern.

Typical decision survey responses for career pattern one

A sample of the types of responses from men and women who are successful in careers that directly involve children is provided for your review. This summary will help you better understand the descriptions of the specific careers that follow.

Step One: Why do you want to work with or for young children?

Question	Typical Response
1. Why do you feel early childhood is an important period of life?	*Early childhood is the time when growth is great and learning rapid. So much of what a young child experiences early affects the quality of later years.*
2. Why do you want to take an active role in shaping young children's experiences?	*Becoming involved in programs and services for young children is the most direct way to contribute to their development. Doing it yourself means it really will get done.*
3. What do you like about young children?	*I like the joy, the innocence, the sense of beginning one has with young children. I like the strong emotions–love, anger, wonder, etc.–that surface as children learn to control themselves and their world.*
4. What do you find challenging and stimulating about young children?	*Children are all different. Each child requires a new approach and each child can teach me something.*
5. What kinds of contact do you enjoy with children and adults?	*I like working directly with children. I like the messes, the hugs, the questions, and even the upsets as we help children cope with their feelings and with others. enjoy cooperating with other adults in working with children.*
6. How do you communicate most comfortably and effectively with children and adults?	*I find it easy to talk about things that interest children in ways that they understand. I appreciate everyday experiences and like to share information about people, places, ideas, and happenings.*

Question	Typical Response
7. When you work hard on something, how often or how quickly do you need to see results?	*I'm generally patient, sensitive to small or subtle indicators of success or enjoyment. I like to try things over again and enjoy variations of familiar activities.*
8. What kinds of help and support do you need to continue working on something over a period of time?	*I generally can work for long periods on something or with someone if I feel the situation is right and all concerned are profitably occupied. I know when I'm doing well at something.*
9. What kind and how much responsibility are you comfortable in assuming?	*I feel confident in accepting responsibility for myself and for supervision of children while providing them with opportunities to grow and learn.*
10. To what extent are you confident about explaining the things you do to others who evaluate you?	*I am willing to explain what I do to my supervisor and the parents of the children I work with. Everything I do is based on my knowledge about and experience with young children.*
11. What sort of things that you do leave you with a good feeling about yourself?	*I really feel I have done something when I help children. I feel useful, needed, and important when I am working with young children.*
12. What kind of image do you want others to have of you?	*I want others to think of me as a caring, concerned individual, someone who can adapt to the requirements of others and strive hard to meet their needs.*

Step Two: What are your skills and abilities?

Question	Typical Response
13. What is your educational background?	Educational requirements vary greatly within this pattern.
14. What specific experiences have you had related to careers with young children?	Individuals in pattern one careers typically have had a broad range of experiences working with young children. The experiences usually show a pattern of increasing responsibility and training with the individual needing less and less supervision of daily activities.
15. What general abilities have you demonstrated in your experiences with young children?	*I can relate well to young children, talking easily and spontaneously with them. I can manage individuals and groups. I find myself helping children extend their knowledge and interests. I can plan and execute appropriate activities for young children in a number of areas.*
16. What abilities have you demonstrated in professional and social experiences with adults?	*I make friends easily and find it rewarding to work with others on shared projects.*
17. What abilities have you demonstrated in your experiences with groups and organizations?	*I contribute to group activities and am reliable and dependable in carrying out responsibilities. I often contribute ideas that others pick up on and carry out.*
18. What initiative abilities have you demonstrated?	*I can plan ahead for activities making sure that all arrangements are confirmed and all materials gathered. I can break down a large task into smaller, sequential, manageable parts. I like to start projects on my own.*

Step Three: What degree of involvement with children is best for you?

Career Pattern	Jobs
1. Jobs that involve working directly with children on a daily or very frequent basis.	Child care aide, Head Start aide, preschool owner, pediatric nurse, family day care provider, babysitter-housekeeper, Head Start teacher, child care worker, school psychologist, pediatrician, speech therapist, physical therapist, school nurse, hospital play aide, infant caregiver, public school teacher, bus driver, nursery school teacher.

Meet the owner, director, and head teacher of a private nursery school

Ann spends most of her time working directly with children as a teacher.

How does a person come to be the owner and director of a private school? To find out, we talked to Ann. She is currently the owner of a private nursery school that employs one other teacher in addition to Ann and enrolls about 20 children in a morning program and another 20 children in the afternoon.

Ann's story is included with career pattern one because she spends most of her time working directly with children as a teacher. She handles her other responsibilities as owner and director at those times when children are not in attendance.

Ann's route to this venture was through the field of music and children's literature. But the experience that had the greatest impact on her decision to open a nursery school was the rearing of her own three children. Ann

described the change from music teacher to nursery school teacher: "When I had my own children I realized I had not been looking at the whole child. I saw that children were learning all the time. They were always wanting intellectual stimulation, needing chances to be creative, moving and active, and interested in expressing emotions. And I thought about how I could learn to do these things with many children—not just my own."

To fulfill her new ambition to learn to deal with the whole child, Ann returned to school. She already had a college degree in music and music education, but she knew this was not enough. Ann was captivated by the match between her ideas about children and those of Dr. Maria Montessori. She found a training program about 50 miles from her home, and after discussing the commitment with her family, she enrolled.

Ann spent her first year following the training program locating space for her own school and adapting it so state requirements for a license were met. Her husband and children played important roles in helping to construct storage areas, furniture, and learning materials. She sought the advice of a lawyer and, with others, formed a nonprofit corporation for reasons of taxation and insurance.

There was considerable financial risk as Ann had to spend several thousand dollars to get the school started, even though she had assessed the available nursery schools in her area and was convinced hers had something very different to offer. Susan was employed as the co-teacher, and together they planned the program, advertised, and interviewed prospective children, and, at last, were ready to begin. For several years, Susan and Ann worked together in a half-day program using rented church facilities. Each year they served

about 20 children ages three to six years old. The need to pack away all materials every Friday so the church Sunday School program could use the facilities became tiresome, and the only solution appeared to be the purchase of a facility and extension of the program. Eventually Ann and her husband located and renovated a suitable house. Ann and Susan are still working together after eight years and are as enthusiastic as ever about their program. The school has grown in reputation, and they can now afford to pay themselves a more adequate salary for their full-time commitment. They see their nursery school as " . . . a time for presenting children with an environment that has stability, consistency, challenge, and patterning . . . a place for quality time for the preschool years . . . a chance to help children gain a good base for their later life."

Most of their efforts are concentrated on planning individual programs and actually working with the children. But their duties also include such everyday things as vacuuming, preparing juice, mending materials, weeding the garden, etc. Ann, as the director as well as a teacher, must also purchase materials, handle financial matters, meet with prospective families, advertise the program, have school forms printed, and handle records of children's progress. She is also responsible for keeping up to date on state and local certification, licensing, and zoning requirements.

Ann's daily schedule is a full one. She arrives at school about 8:30 a.m. (one-half hour before any of the children arrive). Usually she brings some project she worked on the previous evening. She may have prepared some special teaching material for an individual child or repaired the puppet theater or mixed up a new batch of play dough.

When she arrives at school, Ann makes a quick check around the rooms

As the director as well as a teacher, Ann must purchase materials, handle financial matters, and maintain records.

to be sure all the materials are ready for the day. She sets out a special activity for each child the afternoon before, so her morning is not a time of frantically getting ready. She and Susan often have ten minutes or so for a cup of coffee and a leisurely chat about what each of them is doing before the arrival of moms, dads, and children. Ann and Susan stay near the door during arrival time because they value the daily contacts with parents.

During the first hour and a half or so, all of the children are engaged in free choice activities such as looking at books, doing puzzles or instructional games, working with clay or paint, building with blocks, using puppets, listening to records, drawing, using the props and pretending in the housekeeping center, woodworking, and what seems like a hundred other things! While they go about these activities rather independently, Ann takes a few minutes to work individually with each child on a specially selected learning task. Often these tasks are Montessori materials and lessons. She keeps meticulous records in a daily log about each child's performance.

Sometimes the entire group embarks on a project such as a walk in the neighborhood to find leaves, a trip in the snow to scatter seed for the birds, or planting both flowers and vegetables in the garden. Sometimes there is a special cooking project, or a parent may visit to show slides of a family's trip.

About 10:30 a.m., the group gathers for storytelling, dancing, movement experiences, or music (sometimes a little of all of these). Ann's group is often joined by Susan and her group of eight or so younger children. Following this, there is time for a snack, and the chil-

dren are responsible for pouring, serving, and cleaning up. A time for stories and quiet conversation ends the morning. The first parents begin arriving at about 11:25 a.m., and the last child is usually on the way home by 11:40 a.m.

Ann and Susan have made a firm agreement about using the lunchtime from 11:45 a.m. to 12:15 p.m. for relaxation rather than work. They set up quickly for the afternoon children, since the morning children have cleaned up after themselves. The afternoon group of children begins arriving about 12:25 p.m., and the morning schedule is repeated for this new group of children from 12:30 to 3:00 p.m.

After the last child leaves around 3:10 p.m., there is still much to be done. All of the learning tasks and related materials for both morning and afternoon children have to be planned and set up. This is usually done on a weekly basis with minor adjustments

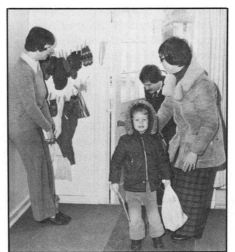

Ann stays near the door during arrival time because she values the daily contact with parents.

each day depending on what has been recorded in the log about the child's performance. Sometimes there will be a parent conference, or parents who are considering the school may set up an appointment to talk with Ann.

Ann and Susan find that their own personal and family lifestyles have become intertwined with the activities of the school. Often their families help make teaching materials or volunteer for something. It is hard for either of these teachers to separate their school commitment from their family life.

They are both active in their local Affiliate Group of NAEYC, and Ann has just finished a successful year as program chairman. The group meets at various schools in the area and can observe aspects of other early childhood programs. All members look forward to the arrival of *Young Children* and often order books and materials advertised in the journal.

Neither Ann nor Susan are required to continue their educations since they are both fully certified teachers, but they regularly take advantage of evening courses or summer programs to extend and refine their skills. Ann is especially interested in learning how to better deal with handicapped children. She and Susan find plenty of intellectual stimulation as they share new ideas and together seek solutions to problems. As Ann said when we asked her if she ever got bored being around children all day, "Who me? You must be kidding! Every one of these children represents a fresh new challenge each and every day."

Both Ann and Susan are quick to point out that their knowledge of child development and early childhood program practices is essential. They also see a need to be systematic and have their time well budgeted. But, in the final analysis, they say that it is the personal attributes that are really important in teaching. Their list includes: warmth, sensitivity, satisfaction, security, patience, high energy, sense of humor, liking children, and the acceptance of the individuality of each child.

When asked what their future plans were, Ann and Susan talked about the never-ending joy and challenge of working with young children, "We see the preschool years as quality time for children. If we help each child gain a good skill foundation and a strong self-image, we know they will do well in the larger world."

Meet the aide in a Head Start program

Louise is an aide in a Head Start program that serves a group of four-year-olds. Most of the children come from low-income families, and situations within the family often make the children's lives difficult. Louise needs every ounce of patience and love she can muster when she is with this lively group from the time they arrive at 9:00 a.m. until they depart for home after lunch, about 1:00 p.m. During the four hours or so she spends with them, Louise finds herself assisting in many homelike tasks with children—feeding,

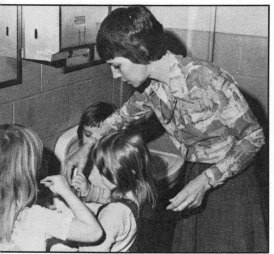

Louise finds herself assisting in many homelike tasks with children. But there is a lot more to her job.

clothing, toileting, toothbrushing, etc. But there is a lot more to her job: Louise has responsibility for guiding these children's learning as she works alongside the teacher in the Head Start classroom. She is usually not responsible for planning learning activities, but she must take the initiative to see that the day's plans run smoothly.

To an outsider, much of what Louise does would not seem like teaching, but anyone who observed the children's progress over a period of several months would be convinced that she was doing a lot of informal teaching. The Head Start classroom looks much the same as other early childhood classrooms. There is a sand table and an area for water play. The block area

includes building blocks as well as props for dramatic play and wheeled toys. There is a housekeeping center with furniture and household equipment, a comfortable place to go and browse through books, easels and clay and other art media, puzzles and other games and materials, and an outdoor play area. Louise moves around this entire area to keep on top of what is going on throughout the room. The children are encouraged to make choices for themselves, and when it is time for free play, there is no need for any direct teaching unless some children need adult help with a problem. How does she get in so much teaching? Louise is quick to take advantage of a situation to point out something new to a child, or she is there when she is needed to demonstrate a part of a game or to comment on an art project. She is also available when friends are having trouble playing together and an adult needs to help them sort out their feelings; she is a lap to sit on during a story, someone to pretend to be a police officer during an outdoor traffic game, and the person who puts the stars on the toothbrushing chart. She describes herself as a happy person who feels in control of each situation. She thinks the most important qualities she brings to her job as an aide are patience, love of children, and, above all, common sense.

Looking back on her life, Louise is surprised she ended up with a paying job. She had always thought of herself as a wife and mother and never considered she would want or need to work outside of her own home. As a teenager she babysat a great deal and had always genuinely enjoyed the children. She had served as a Sunday School teacher for her church and a family day care provider in her home after her children were in school. The families whose children she was caring for moved away from the area at about the same time, and Louise was left without any young children in her life. Gradually she realized that she truly missed this contact and started to look around informally for a job that would include frequent and direct contact with young children.

Louise has a high school education and has had the benefit of the Head Start career development training programs since she has been employed as

an aide. She has one full day of in-service training each month and several other periods of staff training during the year. She feels very confident in her work with the children, but she sees that her confidence and skills have grown remarkably since she first started as an aide in the Head Start program three years ago.

When asked what advice or guidance she would give to others considering similar types of employment, she said, "Well, you know, lots of people don't like to take orders from anybody else. I know I'm not the teacher here. I know I'm not in charge, but I'm the kind of person who is not bothered by that sort of thing. I can see that Mrs. Boxwell, the head teacher, gives me more responsibility each year. But, she only did that after she knew I could handle it. I'm proud of that—proud to think that I have learned about how children behave and how I can work better with them." Louise is such a caring person. It hurts to think a child is suffering, and she feels so helpless sometimes. She knows that the children and families are being helped although their development is sometimes very slow and painful. You have to look carefully to see changes, but they are there. In her words, "If you can give that child the desire to learn at the beginning, you have done something important. You can help children develop a love of school and an enjoyment for learning."

Louise moves around to keep on top of what is going on throughout the room.

Meet the pediatric nurse at work in a hospital outpatient clinic

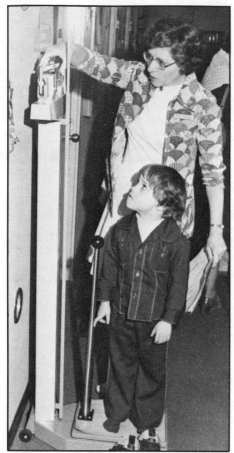

Much of the work in the pediatric clinic consists of routine physical examinations with well children.

Joyce is a pediatric nurse who works with a team of pediatricians, pediatric specialists, and other nurses in a hospital clinic. We interviewed her during her lunch hour on an especially busy day. She told us that many other men and women who are pediatric nurses were at work in the hospital, but they were working in the wards with children who were hospitalized. Some of the children Joyce works with are quite ill, but they can be seen in the clinic as outpatients. The pediatric nurses who work in the hospital wards work the standard shifts of other hospital personnel. Because Joyce's job is different, she works a schedule of 8:30 a.m. to 5 p.m., five days a week.

Joyce explained that the training for a pediatric nurse varies slightly from state to state. Completion of a nursing training program and licensing as a registered nurse (R.N.) is required. Beyond that, no special training is necessary although a college degree in nursing with an emphasis on pediatrics is very helpful. All nurses in training get experience in pediatrics as a regular part of their rotation through the various services of a hospital.

Joyce has a bachelor's degree in nursing and an R.N. license in two states. When asked to tell about training experiences that had proven especially helpful, Joyce replied, "Certainly courses in pathology of children's illnesses and child development were most beneficial. Also, courses in psychotherapy and guidance have helped me. These courses were *all* electives. I wanted to be a pediatric nurse from the beginning and selected courses I felt would provide me with the expertise to be a good pediatric nurse." Joyce said that her experience as an aide in a pediatric ward as a high school student made her aware of areas that a pediatric nurse needed more than a typical R.N. program with courses in psychology, chemistry, biology, physiology, nursing methods and practices, human development, and health. They are necessary but need to be augmented with specifics about children.

Joyce explained that she has been seriously considering taking advanced training to become a nurse practitioner (nurse associate in some states). It is not required in her current job, but she feels she could be much more useful in the day-to-day work in the pediatric clinic since a nurse practitioner can perform routine physical examinations in place of the doctor, and so much of the work in the clinic consists of such examinations with well children. A friend, Sarah, has completed such a training course and is now at work in a new and very exciting area of nursing. Most nurse practitioner programs in the United States require about one year's work beyond the bachelor's nursing degree, although all such programs are not coupled with a master's degree.

Sarah is a member of a multidisciplinary team dealing with child abuse in a countywide area. She works mainly with young parents who are having difficulty dealing with their roles and responsibilities as parents. Some of the children require direct nursing care, and this is almost always delivered in the home. Much of what Sarah does each day, though, is in addition to direct nursing care. She finds herself spending much of her time interacting with the families in their homes as a counselor, teacher, and resource person. She told us, "Sometimes I can get results on an informal basis when the social workers are not able to make any headway. I think this is because the families see me as someone who does not have any real authority or punitive power. I could not, for example, take the children out of the home as social workers, working through the courts, could. So I think the parents are less afraid of me and maybe more willing to be open in discussing their problems."

We asked Joyce to think about the reasons for choosing pediatric nursing as a career. Originally, Joyce chose nursing because she was attracted to doing something in the sciences but recognized that she was also basically an idealistic person. She did not see that she would be very happy as a scientist at work in some laboratory, perhaps dealing with problems that had very little payoff for human welfare, at least in the immediate future.

Joyce discovered that children usually get well faster than adults, and she enjoyed being a part of their rapid recovery. She also discovered that when a nurse works with children, she has numerous opportunities to work with families. Joyce thinks that this interest in the entire family unit, which she recognized as part of pediatric nursing, eventually led her to her present position. In this situation, she deals directly with at least one of the parents when children are brought to the clinic.

Joyce really seems to have a firm grasp on her personal feelings about nursing. She has been outspoken about some of the usual practices in pediatrics, and feels strongly that children need an advocate within the health care system. She said she had seen children pushed or treated mechanically by many doctors, nurses, and even parents, when it comes to health care. She feels children need someone with real warmth, understanding, and skill to be there with them, working for them. "Not just to see if the correct procedures are being used, but to see that things that affect the individual's affective and psychosocial needs were being considered," she said.

Joyce's busy day consists of recordkeeping, informal teaching of good health care while talking with parents, assisting the pediatricians, doing routine tests, and data collection such as height and weight measures, blood pressure, etc. She also carries out the physician's orders—giving medication and injections, assisting in minor surgical procedures, and arranging for followup visits to other specialists.

Joyce feels that the pediatric nurse is important as an advocate for the child. The nurse is important in giving the child a positive attitude about health care. "How the child recovers and his or her attitudes about health and self are so influenced by the attitudes and experiences during a childhood disease, illness, or surgical experience. The nurse is important as a teacher of preventive medicine who should be involved in teaching good health practices both in the hospital clinic when the parents are with their children and again in community meetings and in school classrooms with children and parents and teachers."

Joyce feels strongly about preventive medicine and that teaching good health is one of the best medicines. As one way of achieving more success in the preventive medicine aspects of her job, Joyce has helped write a booklet on child development; symptoms of childhood diseases; first aid; and simple, at-home treatment of childhood diseases. The booklet was published by the hospital and is distributed to all the patients in the hospital clinic. Other community groups also publicize and distribute the booklet.

Joyce's daily schedule is very predictable, with the exception that clinic hours are rarely over when they are supposed to be. She has an occasional evening meeting with a community group, but generally speaking, her own family life is not interrupted by the demands of her job too often.

When we asked Joyce to describe requirements for keeping current in the field, she chuckled a bit and said, "Well, as it stands right now, when you are licensed, it's for life. Many of us who are practicing professionals have kept current through our own efforts, but there are no requirements to do so. We have some indications that more stringent requirements for continuing professional development are coming in the near future, and many of us are gearing up to be ready."

She indicated that she belongs to the American Nurses Association, Division of Maternal and Child Health, and the National League for Nursing. She values highly the professional contacts she has made through the professional publications and the local and regional meetings of the groups.

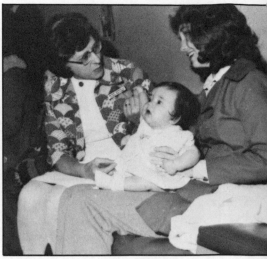

Joyce informally teaches about good health care while talking with parents.

We asked her to sum up what essential qualities she would see in pediatric nursing in addition to the physical caregiving skills. Joyce feels a pediatric nurse must be a warm person, sensitive to the feelings and the interpersonal relationships surrounding the child as a patient in the hospital or the doctor's office or clinic. An ability to communicate freely and sincerely with patient, family, professionals, and staff is crucial. "A good pediatric nurse uses good common sense about people and thinks quickly and acts calmly," according to Joyce.

Look for these men and women at work with children

Family day care providers, housekeepers, babysitters

Family day care providers, housekeepers, and babysitters care for young children when their parents are unavailable. Housekeepers are also responsible for the upkeep of the home and the preparation of meals for the employer's family. While babysitters and housekeepers are usually responsible for one family's children, family day care providers most often care for children from a number of families.

Careers of this type usually do not require formal training. Many of these men and women, although not all, have completed a high school education. While few have formal training related to child care, the majority have the practical experience of raising their own children. There are no entry requirements except the desire to work with young children in this capacity. However, family day care homes must meet certain requirements in order to be licensed, and the family day care provider may be required to have some training in child development and nutrition.

Housekeepers and babysitters usually work in the child's home, while family day care providers work in their own homes. Generally, all people in these positions function independently. There is, however, a growing trend for organizing family day care providers. This network functions as a support system for the providers; it may serve as a contact with community agencies and may have a system of substitutes. Family day care networks frequently provide staff development workshops. The hours of employment vary considerably; however, it is not unusual to work from early morning until early evening.

Typical Schedule for a Family Day Care Provider

Time	Activities	Skills and Attitudes
7:00–8:30 a.m.	Greets children and parents as they arrive; serves breakfast.	Knowledge of nutrition. Sensitivity to children's transition difficulties. Ability to interact comfortably with parents.
8:30–10:15 a.m.	Sets up materials and activities for children. Supervises and interacts with them.	Knowledge of appropriate activities and materials. Ability to interact comfortably with children and to help them learn from their experiences.
10:15–10:45 a.m.	Prepares a snack with the help of children.	Knowledge of nutrition. Appropriate expectations as to the ways children can be involved in food preparation.
10:45–12:00 noon	Supervises and interacts with children during outdoor play.	Awareness of safety hazards. Ability to interact comfortably with children and help them learn from their experiences.
12:00 noon–1:00 p.m.	Prepares lunch with children, serves, and cleans up.	Same as for morning snack.
1:00–3:00 p.m.	Children nap.	
3:00–3:30 p.m.	Prepares an afternoon snack.	Same as for morning snack.
3:30–5:00 p.m.	Supervises children's play. May have some specific activities planned.	Same as other activity period.
5:00–5:30 p.m.	Prepares children to go home. Discusses the day with parents.	Same as arrival.

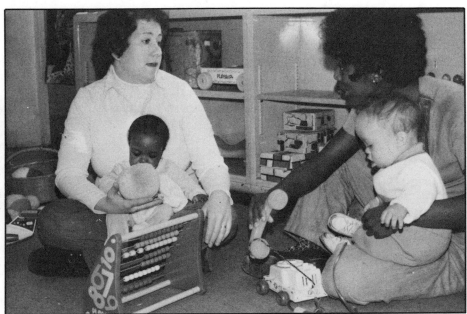

The family day care provider may spend as much time with the child as the parents do and therefore exerts a considerable influence upon the physical, social, emotional, and intellectual development of the child.

All of these positions impact greatly on young children. The family day care provider, housekeeper, or babysitter may spend as much time with the child as the parents do and therefore exerts a considerable influence upon the physical, social, emotional, and intellectual development of the child. Low wages are the norm for these positions. There is generally very little opportunity for advancement other than increases in salary. Because of the increasing number of women entering the labor force, the demand for these positions is expected to increase. Tax allowances for child care expenses may serve to improve wages for this type of work.

Teachers/caregivers

Teachers in Head Start, day care, early childhood programs, kindergartens, and primary grades, teachers of young handicapped children, homebound teachers, and teachers in hospitals are responsible for the education and care of children in a formal setting. While Head Start, day care, and preschool teachers do not need to be college graduates in all states, some coursework in child development and early childhood education is generally required. Most states do require certification or licensing for these positions. All teachers in public school systems or working with handicapped children need to be college graduates, and they need to obtain teacher certification in the state in which they teach.

Classrooms in schools as well as other buildings, day care centers, hospitals, and homes are all settings where teachers and caregivers may be employed. Hours vary depending upon the specific job. Public school teachers usually work six to seven hours a day, five days a week, plus time for extensive preparation. Day care staff generally work eight hours a day and must also spend time in preparation. Preschool and Head Start teachers may only work half days, plus planning time. All of these positions require contact and involvement with parents, often after regular school hours—parent/teacher conferences, parent education classes, and/or home visits. In any of these positions, people may teach throughout their entire career or they may advance to administrative positions. Teachers and caregivers are responsible for a large number of children for their entire work day. They must also keep up with current developments in the field and often take part in in-service training.

Typical Schedule for an Early Childhood Teacher In a Part-Day Program

Time	Activities	Skills and Attitudes
8:30–9:00 a.m.	Preparation of classroom.	Knowledge of appropriate activities and materials to foster learning.
9:00–9:15 a.m.	Greets children and parents as they arrive.	Interpersonal skills in relating to children and adults.
9:15–9:30 a.m.	Group time—discussion of the day's activities.	Ability to interact with children as a group and to clearly present available activities.
9:30–10:30 a.m.	Supervision of children's activities. Active involvement with children, individually and in small groups.	Ability to make activities and experiences meaningful to children. Knowledge of purpose of activities. Appropriate expectations for individuals.
10:30–11:00 a.m.	Supervision of cleanup and hand washing. Snack.	The attitude that children benefit from carrying out responsibilities without too much adult interference. Ability to make snack a pleasant social and learning experience.
11:00–11:30 a.m.	Group time—story, songs, discussion of day's events.	Ability to interact with children as a group and to plan activities that will be enjoyable and meaningful. Skills in helping children reflect on and evaluate their activities and experiences.
11:30 a.m.–12:00 p.m.	Children are picked up by parents. Informal conversations with parents. Clean up classroom.	Skill in conveying information to parents about their children.
1:00–2:00 p.m.	Preparation for next day.	Skill in planning meaningful activities for children. Evaluation of day's activities and each child's progress.

All teachers and caregivers of young children need limitless patience; they need to be well organized; and they must be able to show affection and warmth to children. They need to inspire confidence in both children and parents by projecting an air of assurance, calm, and knowledge. Teachers and caregivers are often children's first major contact with the world outside of their families. The experiences they provide form the basis for the child's later learning.

Competition will be keen for available openings in all teaching areas. However, opportunities will exist for those who are willing to relocate, especially in inner-city areas and rural districts. Men are especially in demand in early childhood education. Public

Teachers are responsible for the education and care of a group of children in a formal setting.

school teachers' salaries vary widely; preschool, day care, and Head Start teachers generally earn considerably less. Public school and many Head Start and preschool teachers are employed for nine to ten months of the year. Day care centers usually operate all year.

Physicians

Physicians are concerned with the physical well-being of children through preventive as well as restorative medicine. The personal qualifications required of a physician are: emotional stability, intellectual curiosity, sound judgment, compassion, coping capabilities, realistic self-appraisal, sensitivity in interpersonal relationships, and physical stamina. Physicians must obtain a bachelor's degree, after which

three to four years of study in an accredited school of medicine are required. Following medical school, a physician will continue his or her education for at least one year as a resident in a post-graduate, hospital-based program. Another one to six years may be required for specialization, such as pediatrics.

Physicians are predominatly self-employed, although they are often affiliated with clinics or hospitals. They may be on constant call and work long, irregular hours. The seriousness of their responsibilities may exert extreme pressure upon them. They must keep themselves informed of new developments in medicine through professional journals, conferences, and training.

A physician's day consists of office hours, hospital rounds, consultation with other health professionals, emergency calls, and updating one's professional information. During office hours, the physician examines patients, diagnoses ailments, administers treatments, and advises patients and/or their parents. During hospital rounds, the physician performs similar tasks; however, in these cases the patients require twenty-four hour care. Some physicians spend part of their hospital hours assisting in surgery. These activities require a knowledge of normal child development, preventive medicine, disease and injuries, pharmacology, and medical therapy. Physicians who work with young children must be empathetic to their fears and concerns and those of their parents.

Physicians impact directly on young children by preventing illnesses, treating them during childhood diseases and injuries, and helping them acquire good health habits and a positive attitude toward health care. Salaries are high for established physicians. There is a continuing need for physicians, especially in rural areas.

School nurses

School nurses are on the front line of prevention and early detection of children's medical problems. They have the same training as other nurses (see section on pediatric nurses, p. 15). Expanding school health programs give nurses increased opportunities to look for early signs of disease, slow development, or malnutrition in school-age children. Additionally, school nurses have a legal responsibility to report possible child abuse cases. They show teachers how to detect health problems in students and may suggest ways to help handicapped children. Nurses help school personnel plan and implement emergency care, physical examinations, immunizations, screening, and hearing and vision tests. They also instruct students about health care.

School nurses perform their services out of an office within the school. They are often assigned to more than one school within a district, and some make home visits. They work the same hours as teachers. The time demands and pressures are often dependent upon the character of the school population and the availability of other forms of medical care.

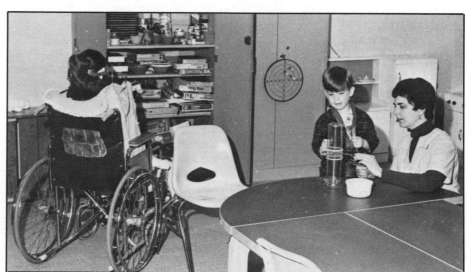

Teachers are employed in Head Start, day care, early childhood programs, kindergartens, primary grades, schools for disabled children, and in hospitals.

Typical Schedule for a School Nurse

Time	Activities	Skills and Attitudes
8:00–9:00 a.m.	Recordkeeping	Ability and interest to keep accurate and current health records.
9:00–10:30 a.m.	Vision screening clinic at school A.	Skills in vision screening. Ability to understand young children's unfamiliarity with this type of activity and their concerns. Skill in communicating clearly with young children.
10:30–10:40 a.m.	Travel to school B.	
10:40 a.m.–12:00 noon	Office hours at school B—seeing children who complain of illness, simple diagnosis, calling parents if necessary.	Skills in early detection of illness. Compassion for and understanding of sick children. Ability to communicate with parents.
12:00 noon–12:45 p.m.	Lunch	
12:45–1:00 p.m.	Travel to school C.	
1:00–2:00 p.m.	Teach class to kindergarten on toothbrushing.	Knowledge of content. Ability to present material in an interesting and effective manner.
2:00–3:00 p.m.	Office hours at school C.	Same as other office hours.
3:00–3:30 p.m.	Preparation for future classes, clinics, etc. Available to teachers, principal. Contact with psychologist, social workers, etc.	Organizational skills. Interpersonal skills in working with other professionals.

School nurses have an advantage over other medical personnel in that they have opportunities for contact with all schoolage children. Because of this, they are a vital link in the health care system. Their work benefits children through the early identification of health problems, through disease prevention efforts, and by helping children develop positive personal health care habits and attitudes. Two factors that influence job opportunities, in opposite ways, are the increased attention to and funding for school health programs and the recent decline in the schoolage population.

Dentist

Dentists examine and treat patients for oral diseases and abnormalities such as decayed and impacted teeth. To an increasing extent, however, modern dentistry is emphasizing education in the proper care of teeth and gums to prevent future dental problems. Most dentists are general practitioners, but about 10 percent are specialists. Two types of specialists have the most contact with young children: (1) orthodontists who straighten teeth; and (2) pedodontists who specialize in dentistry for children. A license to practice dentistry is required in all states. To qualify for a license, a candidate must be a graduate of an approved dental school and pass a state board examination. Dental school training generally lasts four academic years after college undergraduate work. To become a specialist takes an additional two to four years.

Dentists are usually self-employed, although some are affiliated with clinics. They usually have the responsibility of supervising their staff, which may include a receptionist, a dental hygienist, and dental assistants. They must also keep up to date on developments within the profession.

The majority of a dentist's time is spent treating individual patients. This includes examination, actual treatment such as filling teeth, and advising patients as to proper dental care. The dentist may cooperate with schools by performing dental screening and teaching proper dental care. Several hours a week are spent attending to the business aspects of running an office.

The contact a dentist has with children influences their attitude toward care of their teeth and seeking professional care when needed. Employment opportunities and salaries are excellent.

Dental hygienist

Dental hygienists are oral health clinicians and educators who aid the public in developing and maintaining good oral health. They perform preventive and therapeutic services under the supervision of a dentist. A dental hygienist must be licensed by the state where employed. To obtain a license, a candidate must be a graduate of an accredited dental hygiene school and pass both a written and clinical examination.

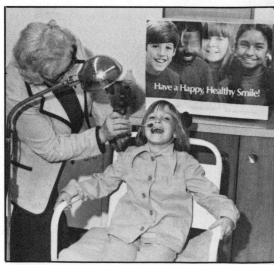

Dentists and dental hygienists spend most of their time working with patients.

Dental hygienists primarily work in dentists' offices, but some work directly with schools, in clinics, or in dental education programs. Their hours will be the same as the office hours of the dentist who employs them.

During a typical day, a dental hygienist may review the scheduled patients' records, clean their teeth, perform preliminary examinations, and prepare the patients for dental work. The hygienist will also instruct the patients in proper care of their teeth and gums and may assist the dentist in performing dental work. Laws defining the specific responsibilities of dental hygienists vary from one state to another. Other factors, such as the size of the office and how the dentist views the dental hygienist's role, also influence the hygienist's specific responsibilities.

Much like a dentist, a dental hygienist is instrumental in forming the child's perception of and habits in personal oral care. Employment opportunities are very good, especially in the area of dental care programs for children.

Physical therapist

Physical therapists help people with muscle, nerve, joint, and bone disease or injury to overcome their disabilities. Many physical therapists specialize in pediatrics and work extensively with disabled children. All states require a license to practice physical therapy. Applicants for a license must have a bachelor's degree from an accredited physical therapy program and must pass a state board examination.

Physical therapists are employed by hospitals, children's clinics, and occasionally by doctors. Some therapists have their own private practice, working in an office or in patients' homes. The hours they work are fairly regular—eight hours a day, five days a week. Time demands and pressures vary, depending on the setting and the ratio of patients to therapists.

Daily activities include many of the following: diagnostic and prognostic testing of the functioning of a patient's muscles, nerves, and joints; planning individualized therapy programs; directing and aiding patients in active and passive muscle reeducation and walking through the use of pulleys, weights, steps, and inclined surfaces;

employing exercise, massage, heat, water, light, and electricity to prevent disability following disease, injury, or loss of a body part; giving instructions in the control of posture; evaluating records and reporting on progress; supervising the work of parents and volunteers; teaching teachers to assist handicapped children. Physical therapists work as members of a medical team that may include physicians, nurses, social workers, and other specialists.

Physical therapists help children overcome physical handicaps and establish patterns of exercise that lead to self-reliance. The employment outlook is favorable with the trend toward earlier recognition and treatment of problems in children.

Speech therapist

A speech therapist identifies speech problems and administers appropriate remedial treatment. The minimum requirement for this position is a bachelor's degree in speech and hearing. Some states require licensing.

Public schools, special private and state schools, and speech clinics employ speech therapists. Some work in private practice. Their hours are usually regular and comparable to other employees in their work setting. The size of their caseload influences the amount of pressure experienced by a speech therapist.

A speech therapist may do any of the following tasks: read doctors' reports; interview the child and parents; examine and test the child; record speech samples; prepare a case history;

analyze and diagnose problems and complaints of the child; prepare and implement the plan for remedial treatment, which could include the use of oral exercises, toy instruments, singing, and other drills and forms of teaching. Speech therapists also interpret results of testing and treatment to teachers and parents and make referrals to other professionals.

Children need to be able to communicate effectively with others, especially through language. Speech therapists assist children who are having difficulties in this area in overcoming their problems. The employment outlook is favorable because of the growing awareness of the need for early recognition and treatment of speech problems in children.

Psychologists and counselors

School, counseling, and clinical child psychologists work with children, their families, and teachers to increase the ability of a child to function within the school and home environment by helping the child overcome behavioral, emotional, or educational problems. Methods used in counseling young children differ in many ways from those used with older people. Professionals in this field need to have personal warmth and ease around adults and children, sensitivity to verbal and nonverbal behavior, and the ability to interact easily with children. Most states require school counselors to have teaching and counseling certificates. Generally, counselors hold master's

A speech therapist identifies speech problems and administers appropriate remedial treatment.

degrees in counseling; clinical psychologists often hold doctoral degrees in psychology.

While their roles are similar, counselors primarily handle early screening, counseling, and initial consultation with parents and teachers. Clinical child psychologists handle more specialized problems in greater depth.

Counselors and school psychologists are employed by school districts or other educational and mental health programs. Their hours are comparable to those of teachers. Student-to-counselor/psychologist ratios are usually very high and therefore create pressure for practitioners. Clinical child psychologists may work with schools, in private practice, or in mental health clinics.

During a typical day, a school psychologist might be involved in the following activities: interviewing and testing a first grader referred for possible learning disabilities, interpreting the tests, maintaining records, and developing an individualized educational plan for the child in conjunction with the teacher; conducting play therapy with a child who is overly aggressive; meeting with the parents of a hyperactive child; testing a child thought to be mildly retarded, confirming the suspected condition, and subsequently referring the child to the special education team. Children encounter complex environments as they mature, and many experience adjustment problems and handicaps of varying degrees. Counselors and psychologists are instrumental in helping them cope with and overcome these problems.

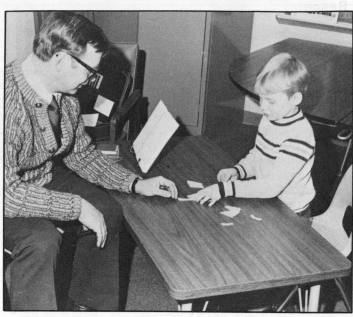

Psychologists work with children, their families, and teachers to increase the ability of a child to function within the school and home.

Conflicting influences are affecting the employment picture. Declining school enrollment and budget problems of school districts have a negative effect on employment. However, recent federal legislation (P.L. 94-142—Education of All Handicapped Children Act) has increased the legal requirement for services as well as funding available to meet the needs of handicapped children. Salaries for counselors and clinical child psychologists are generally higher than those for teaching personnel.

Where do you stand?

Career pattern one includes a wide variety of jobs that require daily or frequent contact with young children. Perhaps some of the jobs described in this chapter interested you. Let's see how you compare with those who have chosen careers working directly with young children.

Take a few minutes to reread each question and your response on the Decision Survey. You may wish to rephrase or add items to some of your responses. Perhaps this section suggested some things to you that you had not thought to record about yourself before. **When you are satisfied with the completeness of your Decision Survey, place it alongside the typical responses in the book and the Rating Sheet. Evaluate the degree to which your responses match the typical responses for this career pattern. Then total your ratings and record the rank of appeal (Step Three, p. 87) you gave to this career pattern.**

When you have completed the rating for career pattern one, you may wish to proceed to the next career pattern, but it is not necessary to complete all five comparative ratings in one session. Guidance in interpreting your ratings begins on page 75.

Resources

ACEI Primary Education Committee. *Let's Be Specific.* Washington, D.C.: Association for Childhood Education International, 1968.

Questions for teachers to ask themselves about philosophy and values in terms of teaching and children and about specific behavior in the classroom.

Almy, M. *The Early Childhood Educator at Work.* New York: McGraw-Hill, 1975.

Descriptions of the functions of professional early childhood educators and the need for working effectively with parents and others.

Andrews, J. D., ed. *Early Childhood Education: It's an Art? It's a Science?* Washington, D.C.: National Association for the Education of Young Children, 1976.

Diverse topics include teacher values clarification, training of pediatricians, and the assessment system of the Child Development Associate Consortium.

Brophy, J. E.; Good, T. L.; and Nedler, S. E. *Teaching in the Preschool.* New York: Harper & Row, 1975.

Discussion of the responsibilities of those who work directly with children in early education settings: administrators, teachers, and paraprofessionals.

The Child Development Associate Credential and the Credential Award System. Washington, D.C.: The Child Development Associate Consortium, 1976.

Descriptions of the role of the Child Development Associate and how to become one. The Credential Award System and the Local Assessment Team and the role of the trainer, the Parent-Community Representative, and the CDA Consortium Representative are also discussed.

Cohen, M., ed. *A Lap to Sit on . . . and Much More: Helps for Day Care Workers.* Washington, D.C.: Association for Childhood Education International, 1971.

A guide for selection and training of teacher aides with suggestions for parent involvement and discussions of the role of men as teachers and creative experiences with dance.

Cohen, M., ed. *That All Children May Learn We Must Learn, Looking Forward to Teaching.* Washington, D.C.: Association for Childhood Education International, 1971.

Twenty articles reprinted from *Childhood Education* that discuss environments, teaching methods, areas for teacher growth, self-evaluation, human relations research, and men in the classroom.

Competency Standards. 2nd ed. Washington, D.C.: The Child Development Associate Consortium, 1975.

A brief description of the Child Development Associate Consortium and the Consortium Credential Award System. Competency standards by which a CDA candidate is judged are divided into six areas.

Duiker, J. W. "Reference List of Paramedical Training Programs in Pediatrics." In *Abstracts of Instructional and Research Materials: Vocational and Technical Education.* (AIM/ARM) Vol. 7, no. 2. February 1973. (ERIC Document Reproduction Service #ED 094 270.)

Information on recognized training programs for pediatric nurse associates, pediatric assistants, and pediatric aides. Includes the program name, institution and director, prerequisites, length of training, and credentials for each type of degree.

Family Day Care: A Self-Portrait. Minneapolis: University of Minnesota, n.d.

A description of family day care in Ramsey County, Minnesota, and the Family Day Care Training Project. Photographs and anecdotes illustrate aspects of working in family day care.

Fogarino, S., and Reynolds, A. *Careers in Child Care.* Washington, D.C.: Day Care and Child Development Council of America, 1974.

Descriptions of jobs and career opportunities in day care centers, nurseries, kindergartens, and family day care homes. Contains questions to ask concerning the necessary characteristics of child care workers and addresses practical considerations such as employment outlook and salary ranges.

Green, M., and Valenstein, T. *The Educational Day Care Consultation Program.* Ann Arbor, Mich.: University of Michigan, 1971. (ERIC Document Reproduction Service #ED 067 157.)

Details of a research and training program for family day care mothers at the University of Michigan.

Headley, N. E. *Education in the Kindergarten.* 4th ed. New York: American Book Co., 1966.

Chapter 4, "The Kindergarten Teacher," discusses personal characteristics of the kindergarten teacher, teacher training, and the teacher's role in the community. Most of the information is applicable to preschool teachers.

Hess, R. D., and Croft, D. J. *Teachers of Young Children.* 2nd ed. Boston: Houghton Mifflin, 1972.

Chapter on "Early Education as a Career" discusses motivations for teaching young children, the social relevance of early education, and career opportunities.

Hildebrand, V. *Introduction to Early Childhood Education.* 2nd ed. New York: Macmillan, 1976.

An overview of early childhood education that covers choosing early childhood education as a career, various types of early childhood programs, the basic philosophy of early childhood education, characteristics of young children, and teaching techniques.

Hipple, M. L. *Early Childhood Education: Problems and Methods.* Pacific Palisades, Calif.: Goodyear Publishing Co., 1975.

Typical problems and situations faced by early childhood teachers. The format is designed for reader response to the situations described. The book also contains information on working with young children, curriculum, equipment and materials, parents, and staff.

Holt, C. L. *Annotated Film Bibliography: Child Development and Early Childhood Education.* St. Louis: Child Day Care Association of St. Louis, Mo., 1973. (ERIC Document Reproduction Service #ED 093 496.)

Film listings suitable for early childhood education teacher training, parent education, and viewing by children.

Howe, R. S. *The Teacher Assistant.* Dubuque, Iowa: Wm. C. Brown Co., 1972.

A guide for teachers in the effective use of the paraprofessional, the book also discusses the professional responsibilities and the specific classroom activities of the teacher assistant.

Howes, V. A. *Informal Teaching in the Open Classroom.* New York: Macmillan, 1974.

Chapter 4, "The Teacher at Work," describes in detail the role of a teacher in an open classroom situation.

Hymes, J. L., Jr. *Early Childhood Education: An Introduction to the Profession.* 2nd ed. Washington, D.C.: National Association for the Education of Young Children, 1975.

The status and problems of kindergartens, nursery schools, Head Start, and child care centers. The final chapter is about the satisfactions involved in working with young children.

Katz, H. P. "Pediatric-Child Psychiatry in a Community Early Childhood Education Center." *Young Children* 28, no. 4 (April 1973): 237-243.

Description of a two-year experience that involved the use of a pediatric-child psychiatry consultant team at an early childhood education center.

Katz, L. G. *Talks with Teachers: Reflections on Early Childhood Education.* Washington, D.C.: National Association for the Education of Young Children, 1977.

Challenges readers to look at themselves as teachers and how they influence children.

Katz, L. G. "Teaching in Preschools: Roles and Goals." *Children* 17, no. 2 (March-April 1970): 42-48.

A distinction is made between teaching role and teaching style. Effects of different teaching styles, the relationship between teachers and parents, and implications for the future are also discussed.

Katz, L. G., and Ward, E. H. *Ethical Behavior in Early Childhood Education.* Washington, D.C.: National Association for the Education of Young Children, 1978.

How can the dilemmas of teaching young children be resolved through a code of ethics?

Kunz, J. T. "The Role of the Nursery School Teacher." In *Nursery School Portfolio.* Washington, D.C.: Association for Childhood Education International, 1969.

Pamphlet describing how the teacher works with children, parents, and other adults.

Lally, J. R.; Honig, A. S.; and Caldwell, B. "Training Paraprofessionals for Work with Infants and Toddlers." *Young Children* 28, no. 3 (February 1973): 173-182.

Description of the Syracuse University Children's Center training program for paraprofessionals. Selection of trainees and types and areas of training are covered.

Moore, S. "The Training of Day Care and Nursery-School Personnel." In *Early Childhood Development Programs and Services: Planning for Action,* ed. D. McFadden. Washington, D.C.: National Association for the Education of Young Children, 1972.

The essential features of a two-year training program for day care and nursery school teachers are described in a paper designed for teaching in a "discovery learning" program that emphasizes cognitive, social, and emotional development.

Murphy, L. B., and Leeper, E. M. *More Than a Teacher.* Washington, D.C.: U.S. Government Printing Office, 1970. DHEW Publication No. (OCD) 73-1027.

Discusses the role of a teacher in terms of mothering. Mothering is viewed as different from mother love, its purpose being to fulfill emotional and physical needs as well as help in social development and building language ability.

Pitcher, E. G., and Ames, L. B. *The Guidance Nursery School.* rev. ed. New York: Harper & Row, 1975.

The section on "The Teacher" deals with the personal qualities of a good teacher, preservice training for teachers, and staff relationships.

Rose, I. D., and White, M. E. *Child Care and Development Occupations: Competency Based Teaching Modules.* Washington, D.C.: U.S. Government Printing Office, 1974.

Module 2: "Finding and Keeping a Job."
Level 1 discusses preparation of personal data for job interviews as well as understanding employee-employer relationships. Level 2 deals with understanding job responsibilities, knowing employment opportunities, and managing personal financial resources.

Module 3: "Understanding Self and Others."
Occupational success is discussed as it relates to self-understanding and interpersonal skills.

Module 4: "Communication Skills."
Listening, oral communication, body language, reading, and writing are all considered communication skills to be developed.

Module 5: "Child Growth and Development."
Outlines normal physical, social, emotional, and intellectual growth patterns for infants through six years of age. Developmental differences are also discussed.

Module 6: "Infant Care."
Training in the provision of quality care for infants, including recordkeeping, activities, providing for physical and emotional needs, and licensing standards.

Module 7: "Toddler Care."
Emphasis on learning the capacities, behaviors, and learning experiences that are normal for toddlers by studying, observing, and working with them. Also discusses relating to the child's family in a positive way.

Module 8: "School-Age Care."

School-age care includes children from six to fourteen years of age. The child care/development worker must be aware of developmental stages and be competent in planning, organizing, and carrying out distinct programs for each developmental level. Parent involvement and community resources are also covered.

Module 9: "Observing and Recording."

Outlines opportunities for the trainee to practice observing, recording, and reporting techniques in order to learn about and understand young children.

Module 10: "Guidance."

Helps the child care worker develop an understanding of the continuous guidance, both direct and indirect, that goes on in child care. Teaches positive guidance techniques.

Module 12: "Child Health and Safety."

Emphasizes the role of the child care worker as a model for good health and safety practices. Maintaining a safe and healthy physical environment for child and legal responsibilities are also covered.

Module 13: "Art"

An exploration of the creative uses of art materials as tools to stimulate children in all areas of growth and development.

Module 14: "Music."

Designed to help students gain skills in using a variety of musical activities and skills in helping encourage young children's spontaneous musical activities.

Module 15: "Dramatic Activities."

Development of an understanding of dramatic play and its value and the ability to encourage and plan for dramatic experiences.

Module 16: "Social Activities."

Helps the child care worker gain experience and skill in guiding the social development of children.

Module 17: "Language and Literature."

Designed to help the child care worker assist young children in language development through modeling good language patterns and appreciating and enjoying good literature.

Module 18: "Science."

Development of an understanding of the kinds of science-related experiences appropriate for preschool children and planning for such experiences.

Module 19: "Pre-Number Activities."

Experiences in preparing and presenting meaningful early number concepts.

Module 22: "Foster Family Care."

Formalized training guide for foster parents.

Module 24: "Exceptional Children."

Provides knowledge of various ways to help disabled children.

Module 25: "Family Child Care."

Training of family child care parents and their self-improvement.

Spodek, B. *Teaching in the Early Years.* 2nd ed. Englewood Cliffs, N.J.: Prentice-Hall, 1978.

A foundation for curriculum and teaching in nursery, kindergarten, and primary years, including subject areas of the school program, classroom organization, techniques of working with parents and children, evaluation, and programs for children with special needs.

Sunderlin, S., ed. *Aides to Teachers and Children.* Washington, D.C.: Association for Childhood Education International, 1968.

Chapters on the role of the aide, training programs, effective work techniques, and the rationale for including aides in the classroom.

Todd, V. E., and Hunter, G. H. *The Aide in Early Childhood Education.* New York: Macmillan, 1973.

A handbook for aides working with young children with descriptions of the role of an aide and suggestions for specific activities to be used in the classroom along with a rationale for each activity.

Films*

. . . And So They Learn (PDE) 1972. 35 minutes, color.

Four approaches to early childhood education: a modified Bereiter-Engleman approach, a team-teaching kindergarten, a Montessori school, and a one-teacher public school classroom. It is pointed out that each method can be effective, depending on the pupils and the learning situation, and that the methods are basically similar.

Approaches to Early Childhood Curriculum (ADL) 1968. 25 minutes.

Three short sequences at preschool level are used to explain the Institute for Developmental Studies' method for teaching abstract concepts, self-image development, and how games can reinforce learning. Martin Deutsch examines the teacher's techniques, successes, and failures.

Child of the Future: Parts I and II (C/MHF) 1966. 57 minutes.

Teaching techniques that give children personal involvement in the subjects they are learning, allow children to be individuals, and speed up the learning process.

Children in the Hospital (IFB) 1962. 44 minutes.

Emotional responses of four-to-eight-year-olds at Boston City Hospital to the stress of hospitalization, illness, and separation are included. Varying defense mechanisms and supportive help that one child can give another are described. Social group work, importance of the attendant volunteer, nurse, physician, and parent are illustrated.

Community Nursery School (NYU) 1965. 40 minutes.

Establishment and operation of a cooperative nursery school, showing the children in significant incidents and relationships among themselves and with the participating parents and teachers.

Day Care Today (PF) 1973. 25 minutes, color.

Illustrates three different types of day care centers (infant, factory, and university-based) and shows how they are responsive to the needs of the children and parents they serve.

*Film distributors are coded and immediately follow the name of the film; see Appendix 1 for complete name and address of distributor.

Development of the Child: Cognition (HR) 1972. 30 minutes, color.

Addresses problem solving in terms of perception, memory, evaluation, and reasoning. Overview of Piaget's theory of intellectual development is included.

Development of the Child: Infancy (HR) 1972. 20 minutes, color.

Behavior and cognitive patterns in the first eighteen months of life are presented. Child's immediate ability to respond to basic sensations, concepts of attachment, stranger and separation anxiety, object permanence, and individual differences are included.

Development of the Child: Language Development (HR) 1972. 20 minutes, color.

Topics included are: child's language processes in the first four years, development of phonemes, syntax, and semantics, process by which language is acquired and how acquisition can be influenced.

The Exceptional Child (TLMD) 1967. 51 minutes.

Exceptional children include the gifted, those suffering from neurological difficulties, the dyslectic, and the stutterer. What causes these conditions and how disabilities should be treated are topics included.

The Humanity of Teaching (MFF) 1974. 27 minutes, color.

Suggests ways of avoiding role stereotyping, being creative as a teacher, and sharing ideas with staff as possible means of developing a humanistic way of dealing with children.

Is a Career in the Health Services for You? (COF) 1970. 14 minutes.

Occupations in patient care and supporting services are described. Various job locations, such as medical centers, mobile units and employment prospects and training required are described.

Kindergarten (C/MHF) 1963. 22 minutes.

A description of typical social development and learning experiences in kindergarten.

The Preschool (PC) 1973. 22 minutes, color.

A day's visit to a preschool illustrates the positive learning environment and long-term benefits that can result from preschool education. An introduction by the California State Superintendent of Public Instruction.

Somebody Waiting (UC) 1972. 24 minutes, color.

This film is about caring for hospitalized children with severe cerebral dysfunction. Effects of appropriate environmental stimulation and therapeutic handling of these handicapped children are described. Hospital staff describe the changes in their personal and professional growth with new methods.

Working with Children: A Commitment to Caring (PMF) 1978. 4 filmstrip sets, sound and color.

Set 1: Understanding the Responsibilities of Child Care; Set 2: Encouraging Healthy Development in Children; Set 3: Dealing with Daily Situations; Set 4: Cooperation among Staff, Family, and Community.

Things to do

Volunteer or paid work with children. Seek out practical experience working with young children in schools, camps, playgrounds, hospitals, day care programs, homes, etc.

Visit and observe programs. Make arrangements to visit local programs that serve young children. Try to get an idea of the many different settings in which young children are cared for.

Take courses about young children. Select courses that focus on young children, their development, and programs. You may find such courses through home economics, psychology, education, or social work in county extension service offerings, or classes in high schools, local college, university or vocational schools.

Read about jobs and interview people. Gather as much information as you can concerning the jobs in which you are interested.

People to talk with

Guidance counselor. A counselor can help you assess your career decision and plan a feasible course of action to prepare for and enter your chosen career.

People working with children. Find someone who *is* involved in a career you think you would like. Ask that person about their training, interests, and job satisfactions.

Parents and relatives. Your parents or other close relatives can often help you make realistic educational and financial plans for your career.

2 Serve Families Directly

Career Pattern Two

Career pattern two includes individuals whose daily work is focused on delivering services to families, although contact with young children in these families may be frequent as well. These services can affect the quality of life for all members of the family unit including young children. Professionals are committed to working through parents to help children, and much of their efforts focus on helping adults realize their potential.

Most careers in this pattern require a moderately high degree of professional training. Individuals who are employed to deliver services to families must be capable of working directly with families as well as working within the agencies and organizations that provide services. Some of the careers found in pattern two are social caseworker, family therapist, educational specialist in a prenatal clinic, parent educator, clergy member, and home economics extension agent.

Individuals can often increase the amount of contact they have with families of young children by specializing. Thus, a social worker could work primarily on adoptions; a public health nurse may work with child abuse cases; or a clergy member may work through a community mental health center counseling grandparents who are raising second families.

Typical decision survey responses for career pattern two

An interest in children within the context of the family setting characterizes careers that cluster under pattern two. Similarities in the many careers included in pattern two can be seen by the typical responses from men and women who work in pattern two careers. Review these responses before reading the interviews and descriptions of the careers.

Step One: Why do you want to work with or for young children?

Question	Typical Response
1. Why do you feel early childhood is an important period of life?	*Young children often put a real strain on family relations and family resources. Young families need help and support so that all family members can grow in appropriate ways.*
2. Why do you want to take an active role in shaping young children's experiences?	*Parents have a major effect on children's growth. By helping them, I can help build family situations in which young children can prosper.*
3. What do you like about young children?	*Young children are enjoyable to interact with, but I don't seek out periods of extended contact or responsibility with them. They are filled with potential.*
4. What do you find challenging and stimulating about young children?	*Helping parents handle young children requires creative, thoughtful approaches. Children, especially young ones, can present incredible challenges to parental maturity and resources.*
5. What kinds of contact do you enjoy with children and adults?	*I enjoy working directly with adults. I like to observe and talk with children occasionally.*
6. How do you communicate most comfortably and effectively with children and adults?	*I find it easy to talk to adults. I am a good listener and frequently ask thought-provoking questions. I respect the values and cultures of others.*
7. When you work hard on something, how often or how quickly do you need to see results?	*While problems may take a long time to be resolved, I expect to see some fairly immediate changes in attitudes and behaviors. When I work hard on something, I like to see others make an effort also.*

---

8. What kinds of help and support do you need to continue working on something over a period of time?

Feedback from others helps me know that I am making a positive contribution. I generally think through situations in advance so that I am fairly certain my actions are reasonable. While I look to others for cues, I can also support myself.

9. What kind and how much responsibility are you comfortable in assuming?

I am willing to analyze and evaluate problems or situations and make recommendations, but the responsibility for action rests with the other person. I am not comfortable running other people's lives for them.

10. To what extent are you confident about explaining the things you do to others who evaluate you?

I am willing to explain what I do to the agencies, services, and families that I work with. I can explain the personal and professional factors that influence my actions.

11. What sort of things that you do leave you with a good feeling about yourself?

I feel good when I have helped others help themselves. It is important to me to work on ways to solve problems, not just immediate solutions.

12. What kind of image do you want others to have of you?

I want others to think of me as a resource to draw on when they have problems they cannot solve themselves.

Step Two: What are your skills and abilities?

13. What is your educational background?

Grade School	
High School	
Associate Degree	
Specialized Training or Certificate	
Bachelor's Degree	x
Master's Degree	x
Doctorate	x
Other	

14. What specific experiences have you had related to careers with young children?

Individuals in pattern two careers typically have experience in working with families or agencies. Experiences with children are common but not as frequent as in pattern one careers.

15. What abilities have you demonstrated in your experiences with young children?

I find it easy to work with young children and their families. I am good at observing small details of people's behavior.

16. What abilities have you demonstrated in professional and social experiences with adults?

Others find me easy to talk with, supportive, and understanding. I often ask questions or give suggestions that others find useful.

17. What abilities have you demonstrated in your experiences with groups and organizations?

I am good at details and making arrangements. I often know just the person who can get the job done when others are still wondering who to ask. I am good at helping others assume and carry out responsibilities.

18. What initiative abilities have you demonstrated?

I can arrange and pace my activities well so that I am not rushed. I think it is important to allow time to interact with others fully.

Step Three: What degree of involvement with children is best for you?

Career Pattern	Jobs

1

2. Jobs that involve helping families provide for their young children.	Social worker, home economics extension agent, public health nurse, education specialist-child care clinic, family therapist, clergy member, parent educator.

Meet the social worker from a community social service agency

It is important for the social worker to get to know each family, assessing their needs and finding services for all the family members.

For information about a career in social work, we interviewed Greta, who is a social worker for a community social service agency. Her major responsibility is to provide direct service to families through working with other professionals in health, education, and social welfare agencies in the community. Greta pointed out that social workers have diverse jobs depending on the location, the major industries, and the population. Greta has a friend who is also a social worker, but her job is quite different since she is the coordinator of family services in a nine-county region. In addition to working directly with some families, this friend spends much of her time training other social workers.

Greta told us that it is important for the social worker to get to know each family, assessing their needs and finding services for all the family members depending on their particular problems or concerns. She is especially interested in seeing to it that the family has resources, so they can, in turn, provide a safe and happy home for the children. She summed up her role as follows, "My concern is really for the total family, their assets, the environment in which they live and, especially,

the overall quality of life for the family." Each family is visited on a monthly basis, and group meetings are conducted for the families in the community service area. Each social worker works with numerous other community agencies to pull together comprehensive services for the families.

There is a great deal of diversity in the problems Greta helps families deal with in an effort to help them become more self-sufficient and able to solve their own problems. For example, one of the families recently experienced a fire in their mobile home. Greta was on the scene almost immediately and helped the family find a place to stay for the rest of the day. Then she arranged for donations of food, furniture, and clothing from other agencies as well as helping the family find temporary housing.

Not all problems have such obvious solutions though. Another of the families Greta sees frequently has a 12-year-old daughter who is a chronic runaway. Greta serves as a resource for psychological services for the daughter and the parents. She works directly with the police on those occasions when the daughter leaves home. Most of all, she is available as a supportive listener in times of crisis, especially for the girl's mother, since the father blames her for the daughter's runaway

Much of Greta's time is spent persuading other agencies to help families.

behavior. It is frustrating to be called on to deal with the same problem over and over again, but Greta understood this aspect of her job from the beginning.

We asked Greta about her educational background and the experiences that led her to social work as a career choice. Greta has a bachelor's degree in speech and a master's degree in social work. Many of her fellow caseworkers do not have master's degrees, and this advanced training is really not required for the position she now holds. Many caseworkers have not had any college training in social work although they usually have a bachelor's degree in some related field. She feels strongly that her background has helped her in many important ways to do a better job.

Much of her time is spent persuading other agencies to help families, and her understanding of group dynamics and public relations has contributed to her success. Even more important than that, at least for Greta, is the experience of raising her own children. As Greta put it, "You know, the textbooks and college courses give you some ideas of what it's like for a family in distress, but, when you have your own children and are coping with some very minor family problems of your own, you really begin to get a feeling of what it must be like to be in real distress. Having had some minor problems of my own to work through, I can feel how desperate some of my families feel. There is no substitute for the experiences of life." Greta would be one of the first to point out that it would be unrealistic to expect everyone to value their own experiences as parents as she does. It is really the ability to empathize that is crucial.

A social worker must be able to feel comfortable being constantly involved in other people's problems. Even though you cannot ever become completely detached, it is necessary to keep emotions under control and work objectively to help families. A social worker has to be a good teacher, because much of the job really involves teaching families more effective ways to meet their own needs and to cope

with their own problems. Another basic skill is to be able to work successfully on a multidisciplinary team.

Part of the responsibilities involved in cooperating with others who serve the needs of children and families is basic knowledge of the social service agencies that exist in a community and a knowledge of their specific services, eligibility requirements, contact persons within the agency, and admissions procedures. Greta said, "You really have to assess the community and identify every possible agency and find out how it works, who is served by the agency, who is not served, and how effective or costly each service is."

Greta recommends that those considering a career in social work take advantage of every opportunity they have to work either directly with families or with children. The opportunities for advancement are not great unless a person is willing to move into more administrative responsibilities. For Greta, this would probably require a willingness to relocate her family since she lives in a rural community now, although caseworkers in larger cities usually have more opportunities for advancement without relocating. Greta is pleased that her family is supportive of her work since she travels extensively throughout the county and often must be away from home in the evenings.

A social worker has to be a good teacher, because much of the job really involves teaching families more effective ways to meet their own needs and to cope with their own problems.

Career Pattern Two

Meet the home economist at work in the county cooperative extension office

Kate is a specialist in informal adult education since most of what she does is teaching and consulting.

What is it like to be a home economist? To find out, we talked to Kate who is the home economist in a county cooperative extension office and part of a team of workers that includes home economists, agricultural agents, and usually one or more youth agents. The major job of the home economist is to work as a resource for the families who live in the county.

Kate's office is in the county seat along with other county offices. Much of her time is spent working with individuals, families, and groups throughout the county providing expertise in a wide variety of topics. These include leadership development, communication, child development, clothing construction and care, home preservation and preparation of foods, home management and home furnishings, family development and family relationships, youth programs and activities, and recreation.

The best way to describe the major role that she has as an extension agent is to think of Kate as a specialist in informal adult education since most of what she does is teaching and consulting. She might:

Join a group of women at their office building cafeteria for an informal workshop on family finances and budgeting during the lunch hour.

Give a talk on family relationships as a guest of the local PTA at one of their monthly meetings.

Arrange and/or conduct a short course on discipline and behavior management for parents under the auspices of the local school district continuing education program.

Serve as a resource for an elementary school teacher who is doing a unit on nutrition.

Work with a Scout troop to set up a workshop on babysitting.

Kate's route to this career was through a bachelor's degree in general home economics. Kate also found that work in psychology, social psychology, and leadership development provided her with basic knowledge helpful in working with people. A master's degree in child development and family relations provided her with even more specialized training.

Some of the experiences in Kate's background that helped her make her decision to become a home economist were her work experiences in social agencies that dealt with children, a summer internship with the cooperative extension service in a neighboring county, camp counseling in the summer during high school and college, and holding leadership positions in high school and college clubs and organizations. Not only had these experiences helped her make her career decision, but she felt these experiences provided her with skills and confidence in herself as she undertook similar activities on the job.

One of Kate's skills that is so necessary to her job is that of oral communication. She must be able to communicate with all types of people in a variety of situations ranging from telephone calls or home visits to speaking to large audiences in auditoriums or appearing on television shows. Writing skills are necessary for communicating through business letters, materials for programs, newsletters, task force reports, and news releases.

Kate described opportunities for advancement on the job. She began as an assistant home economist. The next step was to an associate home economist followed by full or senior home economist. During this time Kate completed her master's degree.

Kate might decide to move to the position of specialist (in clothing, family life, youth, etc.) at a regional level. She would be encouraged to continue graduate work to advance as a specialist. With a doctorate, Kate might be a specialist at a university where she could be involved in teaching and research while serving as a resource and consultant to the county and regional staffs. States have different requirements for each of these positions.

Kate is very involved in professional development. She belongs to the American Home Economics Association, as do most of her colleagues. Because of her special interest in family living, she also is a member of the National Council on Family Relations. She reads professional journals and other publications and also participates extensively in staff development activities.

Kate enjoys her job as a home economist. She enjoys the indirect service to young children that it provides as she works with families and youth in developing knowledge and skills in family living.

Kate was impressed with her high school home economics teacher's interest and understanding of family development and interpersonal relationships. The child development instruction in the classroom was interesting and motivated Kate to read career publications developed by the American Home Economics Teachers Association and the Cooperative Extension Service.

During her college practicum, Kate served as an intern in a county cooperative extension program and found she liked the informal approach to teaching used by the extension agents. The one-to-one contacts over the telephone and occasional home visits with families, trying to answer their questions and provide information about nutrition, home management, childrearing, and child care problems or services were a challenge and also a task she felt the home economist there had handled well.

When asked to describe some of the aspects of the job, Kate was quick to reply, "Oh, you don't want a job as a home economist if you want specific and regular working hours. It is certainly a job that requires a person who is flexible and willing to work varied schedules." Kate went on to describe the necessity of attending many night meetings. Some are held in the county offices, but others are scheduled in homes and community buildings anywhere in the county. Meetings require much travel both within the county and within the administrative region in the state. Numerous weekends are spent participating in or conducting seminars for youth and adults.

Winter is filled with seminars, training and in-service workshops, consultation services with families, and state and national conferences. Summers

Extension agents must be able to communicate with all types of people in a variety of situations ranging from telephone calls or home visits to speaking to large audiences in auditoriums or appearing on television shows.

are spent in camp and youth conference activities, coordinating and setting up summer 4-H projects, training local leaders, giving demonstrations at community and county meetings and field days, setting up contests for 4-H youth groups, and judging contests and setting up exhibits at county fairs.

The focus of Kate's efforts is on families, but she makes an impact in ways in addition to directly serving families. Kate is always on the lookout

for opportunities to be involved in community activities that will eventually influence family life in the community. For example, she serves as a member of the local day care advisory committee.

Kate does not work in isolation as a home economist. She must work in a team with her county staff and with colleagues from other counties, as well as regional and research and teaching specialists at the state university.

Look for these men and women at work with families

Caseworker—child protective services

Child protective services caseworkers are involved in the prevention and detection of child abuse and in the provision of services to endangered or abused children and their families. They represent a life or death intervention for many children and are also an essential element in helping families find better ways of coping with frustrations and other problems. In most states, they are required to have the same educational background as other child welfare employees: a bachelor's degree in social welfare, social sciences, or a related field. Specific skills in family counseling and crisis intervention are necessary. These positions are usually a part of the state or county civil service system.

Child protective services caseworkers generally work out of local or regional child welfare offices. While they

keep regular office hours, they must be available on a twenty-four hour basis to respond to crises. As is typical in all service agencies, caseloads are high, and there is rarely enough time in a day to accomplish all of one's responsibilities. Added to the pressure of time is the fact that much of the work involves dealing with crises in emotion-laden situations.

As these caseworkers are bound by civil service classifications, their salaries will vary. Promotional opportunities are primarily limited to casework supervisor status. Even though there may be a surplus of individuals trained in social services, specialization in child protective services is a new and growing field.

Health educators

The function of the health educator is to give children and adults facts about health and disease so they can act for their own well-being and that of their

families. Health educators are seeking new understandings of human behavior, ways to apply this knowledge in health education, and better approaches to building healthier communities. An increasing number of colleges and universities are now offering a bachelor's degree in community health education. These programs prepare the student for many community jobs as well as graduate study, since leadership positions in this field require a master's degree. This includes training in basic public health areas and in-depth preparation in educational program planning and theory and methods analysis of health education problems.

Health educators are employed by hospitals and county and city government agencies such as health departments and public schools. They work regular office hours and some evenings. Job pressures depend on the character of the population being served and the place of employment.

During a typical day, a health educator will be involved in the planning of community education programs and campaigns, possibly contacting pediatricians to obtain data on the number of children receiving the necessary immunizations. The health educator may work with the schools on setting up an immunization clinic. In the evening, he or she may be the guest speaker at a parent education class on the importance of regular health checkups.

The value a community places on good health is often reflected in the health of its children. A health educator is an important element in making communities aware of their role in providing adequate health care and in making individuals aware of the need to keep themselves healthy. This is an expanding area with a favorable employment outlook.

Parent educators

Parent educators work with parents, usually in group sessions, to help them become more competent in raising their children. Because this is a relatively new field, the requirements for it are flexible, although a bachelor's degree is often required. The base of knowledge needed by the parent educator is interdisciplinary in nature, drawing from the fields of psychology, sociology, anthropology, education, and social work. The parent educator must be sensitive to the concerns of the parents and receptive to their ideas.

A parent educator may be affiliated with a school, college, or university, a family day care network, a day care program, a hospital, or a social service agency. Parent education is usually viewed as an ancillary service to an agency with other primary functions. Programs generally focus on a particular type of parent, such as parents of preschool children, or preparing young people for parenthood. A parent educator may work with one type of program or a variety of specifically focused programs. The parent educator may work during the day, in the evening, or both.

During a typical day, a parent educator will be involved in program

Parent educators work with parents to help them become more competent in raising their children.

preparation and evaluation and in actually conducting sessions with parents. Part of the parent educator's task during these sessions is to translate theory and research into everyday language that parents can use as they relate it to their own lives and actions. A parent educator does more than provide information. His or her main role is enabling the parent's decision-making process; in this way the parent becomes more adept at facilitating the child's learning and development. An understanding of the community's role in meeting individual needs and facility for connecting families with community resources are skills a parent educator uses daily.

Parents are the child's first teachers and the major influence in the child's life. Our increasingly complex and

Time	Activities	Skills and Attitudes
8:30–10:30 a.m.	Recordkeeping, file reports, and other paperwork.	Ability and interest to keep accurate and well-organized records.
10:30 a.m.–12:00 noon	Investigation of possible child abuse. Meet with the family and child at their home.	Knowledge of child abuse laws. Interpersonal skills in working with children and adults.
12:00 noon–1:00 p.m.	Lunch	
1:00–2:00 p.m.	Talk with neighbors of above-mentioned family. Abuse not confirmed.	Ability to make decisions on the basis of available information.
2:00–3:30 p.m.	Conduct group session with potential abusing parents.	Skills in family and group therapy.
3:30–4:00 p.m.	Make followup calls on abuse reports, service referrals, etc.	Skills in working with other professionals.
4:00 p.m.	End of office hours.	
7:45–9:45 p.m.	Receives call on a possible child abuse in progress. Arranges to meet police at the residence. Examines the child. Calms the parents. Discusses with parents the intent to remove the child. Contacts the child abuse shelter. Arranges to meet with the parents the following day.	Ability to be calm in a crisis situation. Interpersonal skills in dealing with upset/angry parents. Knowledge of support services. Knowledge of child abuse laws.
9:45–10:15 p.m.	Transports and enters the child in the child abuse shelter.	Ability to utilize support services effectively.

Typical Schedule for a Child Protective Services Caseworker

changing society serves to make the parental role a difficult and confusing one. Parent educators attempt to help parents with this difficult role and thus improve the quality of the child's life. The employment outlook is favorable since there is a growing awareness that in order to serve children effectively, parents must also be served.

Prenatal and infant parent education

An education specialist in a prenatal or well-baby clinic performs a function similar to that of a parent educator except the focus is on the parents of the infants from conception until the child is about three years old. A bachelor's degree is generally required with course work in child development, early childhood education, and nutrition. Training in nursing or pediatric medicine may also be required. The hours worked are those of the clinic where the specialist is employed. During the course of a day, these men and women counsel expectant mothers on proper nutrition and health care during pregnancy; advise parents on childrearing, normal development, and other areas of concern to parents with the emphasis often on health-related areas; and make referrals to other community resources. The first three years of a child's life are crucial ones. Prenatal education for parents helps to ensure that children are well cared for during these years.

Nurse-midwife

The nurse-midwife is a registered nurse who, by knowledge and skill gained through an organized program of study, is qualified to manage the care of mother and infants throughout the maternity cycle. This program of study must be recognized by the American College of Nurse-Midwives. Nurse-midwifery is currently offered on a post-R.N. or a master's degree level. The post-R.N. program provides a curriculum of theory and clinical experience in nurse-midwifery, while the degree program leads to a master's degree. After completion of studies, one must take the American College of Nurse-Midwives' national examination in order to be certified.

In the United States, a nurse-midwife must be employed by a hospital, clinic, obstetrician, or other medically directed health service. He or she will probably have regular office hours but

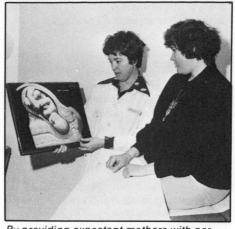

By providing expectant mothers with personal and quality care throughout the maternity cycle, the nurse-midwife has a tremendous impact on the quality of care infants receive from their parents.

must also be available at all times for emergencies and for the onset of labor in patients.

The nurse-midwife's daily responsibilities involve the examination of patients either in their homes or in an office; advising patients on prenatal and postnatal care; managing labor and delivery; and evaluating and providing immediate care for the newborn. The nurse-midwife is prepared to teach, interpret information, and provide support. These duties require interpersonal skills, a sensitivity to the concerns of expectant parents, the ability to remain calm in times of crisis, and reliable knowledge about pregnancy and birth as well as when medical attention is necessary.

By providing expectant mothers with personal and quality care throughout the maternity cycle, the nurse-midwife has a tremendous impact on the quality of care infants receive from their parents. Nurse-midwives are especially in demand in areas where there is a shortage of doctors and by women who desire to deliver their children at home.

Family therapists

Family therapists and clinical psychologists help people with the stresses of everyday living, including those related to marriage and child management. A family therapist needs a bachelor's or master's degree, depending on the licensing requirements of the state. Generally, a clinical psychologist has completed a doctoral program.

Many family therapists and clinical psychologists are self-employed. They may also be affiliated with mental

health clinics or other agencies. They have regular office hours that may include some evenings.

Activities engaged in by family therapists or clinical psychologists include a combination of counseling, teaching, consulting, research, and administration. They try to foster productive problem solving and greater self-awareness. Typically, they work with normal or moderately troubled persons, individually, in groups of adults, with total families, or occasionally with an entire extended family.

Family therapists and clinical psychologists help to improve the quality of the experiences and interactions a child has within the family by increasing each family member's ability to function. Employment opportunities do exist in this field.

Home and school visitors

Home and school visitors serve as a link between the home and the school. A bachelor's degree in education or social work is required; courses in school law, psychology, counseling, and fieldwork are necessary for certification.

Home and school visitors are employed by school districts and must be able to work effectively with both children and adults. They generally work the same hours as teachers, although they may meet with parents during the evening. They usually travel daily within their school districts. Because of the range of responsibilities, time demands and pressures may be considerable.

The responsibilities of a home and school visitor include: consulting with parents about concerns they have regarding their children or families; referring families to community agencies and social services; processing applications for the free and reduced-price lunch program; assisting parents in planning to prevent future truancy or, in the case of illness, making arrangements for homework or referral for home tutoring; and offering support and assistance to pregnant students in their educational planning.

The home and the school environments are influential and important in a child's life. As a liaison between the two, the home and school visitor can serve as a valuable resource to parents, teachers, and children. Salaries are generally comparable to those of teachers in the same school district.

However, the declining school-age population and the financial problems faced by many school districts have resulted in a decline in employment opportunities in the specialty.

Clergy

The clergy function as spiritual leaders in a community, but they are also involved in individual and family counseling, program development, and community work. After high school, those wishing to enter the clergy usually go to college and then a seminary, or they immediately enter a seminary and combine higher education with theological training. Deciding on a career in the clergy involves considerations different from those involved in other career choices. When someone decides to enter the ministry, priesthood, or rabbinate, they do so primarily because they possess a strong religious faith and desire to help others. People considering a career in the clergy should seek the counsel of a religious leader of their faith to aid in evaluating their qualifications.

The majority of the clergy serve their own congregations in churches or synagogues. Some serve as chaplains in the armed forces, industry, correctional institutions, hospitals, or on college campuses. Some serve as missionaries or in social welfare agencies. Most of these positions are twenty-four-hour-a-day jobs. Civic, social, and recreational activities of members of the clergy, as well as responsibilities, often are influenced and restricted by the customs and beliefs of their religion.

When a family is experiencing difficulties, they may turn first to their clergy. The clergy who serve in community churches and synagogues have the most impact on families. Much of their day is spent in individual and family counseling, meeting with church and community groups, preparing sermons, and visiting members of their congregation at home, in hospitals, or in prisons. As a spiritual leader, a member of the clergy may aid children and adults in clarifying their values and in decisionmaking. They need to be sensitive to the needs of others and to be able to help them deal with their problems. The job demands an ability to speak and curate effectively, to organize, and to supervise others. It also demands considerable initiative and self-discipline.

Where do you stand?

Perhaps some of the jobs described in career pattern two interested you. Let's see how you compare with those who have chosen careers working directly with families of young children.

Take a few minutes to reread each question and your response on the Decision Survey. You may wish to rephrase or add items to some of your responses. When you are satisfied with its completeness, evaluate the degree to which your responses match the typical responses (p. 27) for this career pattern. Follow the instructions on the Rating Sheet to record your responses. When you have completed the rating, you may wish to proceed to the next career pattern.

Resources

Bloedorn, J. C., et al. *Designing Social Service Systems.* Chicago: American Public Welfare Association, 1970.
Models for delivery of social services in local communities. Definition of roles and description of services provide an overview of available careers.

Cooperative Extension. *Extension Home Economist.* Moravia, N.Y.: Chronicle Guidance Publications Occupational Brief #192.
Descriptions of the role and responsibilities of the Extension Home Economist for the Federal Cooperative Extension Service.

Datta, L. *Parent Involvement in Early Childhood Education: A Perspective from the United States.* Washington, D.C.: National Institute of Education, 1973. (ERIC Document Reproduction Service #ED 088 587.)
A comprehensive review of parent involvement in early childhood programs. An excellent bibliography for those interested in further study in parent education.

Elliot, D. L. "Needed: A New Early Childhood Educator." *Educational Leadership* 28, no. 8 (May 1971): 835-839.
According to the author, early childhood educators must think in terms of a broader educational context in providing services to young children.

Goldberg, T. "Social Work Students in Day-Care Settings." *Children* 14, no. 3 (June 1967): 113-116.
The placement of social work students in day care centers in New York City. The student's role, especially his or her relationship with the teacher, is discussed.

Gordon, I. J. "The Florida Parent Education Early Intervention Projects: A Longitudinal Look." Gainesville, Fla.: University of Florida, 1975. (ERIC Document Reproduction Service #ED 100 492.)
Information on rationale, procedures, and effectiveness of the program.

Gottlieb, D., and Heinsohn, A. L. *America's Other Youth: Growing Up Poor.* Englewood Cliffs, N.J.: Prentice-Hall, 1971.
A collection of writings related to understanding the lives, attitudes, and social conditions of poor youth in the United States—Puerto Rican, migrant, Mexican-American, Native American, Appalachian, and Black. Careers of those working closely with these children can be related to the readings.

Greenberg, P. "Seminars in Parenting Pre-schoolers." In *Early Childhood Education: It's an Art? It's a Science?* ed. J. D. Andrews. Washington, D.C.: National Association for the Education of Young Children, 1976.

Detailed description of the characteristics a discussion leader needs to conduct a parent education seminar. Also highlights techniques that contribute to the success of such a program.

Hall, A., and Paolucci, B. *Teaching Home Economics.* New York: John Wiley & Sons, 1970.

Descriptions of various programs and definition of the role of the home economics teacher in various aspects of the job.

Honig, A. S. *Parent Involvement in Early Childhood Education.* Washington, D.C.: National Association for the Education of Young Children, 1975.

Descriptions of the ways parents are involved in early childhood education programs and suggestions for parent educators. The resource list is especially helpful for practitioners.

Kahn, A. J. *Social Policy and Social Services.* New York: Random House, 1973.

Social services in today's society and the issues in delivery of these services. The variety of career opportunities can be seen as various services are described.

Leichter, H. J., ed. *The Family as Educator.* New York: Teachers College Press, 1974.

Papers related to issues in the field of parent education provide a look into the future for the field.

Maas, H. S., ed. *Research in the Social Services: A Five-Year Review.* New York: National Association of Social Workers, 1971.

A comprehensive review of the research in the field of social work.

Peters, A. D. "Health Support in Day Care." In *Day Care Resources for Decisions,* ed. E. H. Grotberg. Washington, D.C.: Office of Economic Opportunity, n.d.

The history of health support services in day care, research findings, and current practices.

Pickarts, E., and Fargo, J. *Parent Education: Toward Parental Competence.* New York: Appleton-Century-Crofts, 1971.

A comprehensive treatment of the rationale for parent education and the roles that parent educators assume.

Pisapia, M. L., and Hanwell, A. F. "Social Work in Day Care." *Child Welfare* 48, no. 5 (May 1969): 268-272.

Description of a project that tested methods of assessing the value of social work services as an adjunct to day care programs.

Rich, D. "Helping Parents Become Better Teachers." In *Aides to Teachers and Children,* ed. S. Sunderlin. Washington, D.C.: Association for Childhood Education International, 1968.

A parent education program that teaches parents how to supplement the school at home.

Rose, I. B., and White, M. E. *Child Care and Development Occupations: Competency Based Teaching Modules.* Washington, D.C.: U.S. Government Printing Office, 1974.

Module 11: "Child Nutrition."
Provides a working knowledge of the basic principles of nutrition and skill in applying them.

Module 21: "Working with Parents."
Skills necessary to establish and maintain a positive relationship with parents.

Smith, M. M. "How Could Early Childhood Education Affect Families?" *Young Children* 33, no. 6 (September 1978): 6-14.

Reaffirms the challenge to assure children of the right to opportunities that will facilitate their growth and development. The need for cooperation between families, communities, and the helping professions.

Stevens, J. H., Jr. "Parent Education Programs: What Determines Effectiveness?" *Young Children* 33, no. 4 (May 1978): 59-65.

Characteristics of parent education programs that have led to success. A look at the future.

Vines, C. A., and Anderson, M. A., eds. *Heritage Horizons Extension's Commitment to People.* Madison, Wisc.: *Journal of Extension,* 1976.

The roles and responsibilities of those who work in the Federal Cooperative Extension Service.

Warren, R. L. *Studying Your Community.* New York: Free Press, 1965.

A handbook to describe and analyze the various units found in a community. Specific sections of relevance to careers in early childhood:
Chapter 11: "Aids to Family Living and Child Welfare"
Chapter 12: "Health"
Chapter 13: "Provision for Special Groups"
Chapter 16: "Associations"

Whitesides, B. "The Brookline Early Education Project." *Young Children* 33, no. 1 (November 1977): 64-68.

A successful program for families with young children. Includes pediatric services, home visits, and other parent services.

Woods, T. L. "Social Work Consultation and Student Training in Day Care Centers." *Child Welfare* 22, no. 10 (December 1973): 663-668.

Social work functions in a day care center and the opportunities available in day care centers and nursery schools for social work training.

Films*

Children in Peril (XEP) 1972. 22 minutes, color.

This film deals with child abuse and shows what is being done to prevent it through work with abusive families.

Jobs for You: It's Happening in Home Economics (AHEA) 1972.

This is a filmstrip and record to acquaint high school students of job opportunities available to people with interest and training in home economics. A specific section of the filmstrip deals with community services and child care services. Produced by Guidance Associates.

The People Profession: Careers in Home Economics (GA). Sound, color, filmstrip.

Interviews with home economists working in extension service, child development, business, finance, consumer service, interior design, communication, education, and community service. Produced by the Production Group, a division of Guidance Associates.

Social Worker (UEVA) 1967. 17 minutes.

How the concern of the social worker is reflected in service to people as individuals, as families, in groups and communities is documented.

What Are We Doing to Our Children? Part I—Locked Up: Locked Out (CAF) 1973. 30 minutes, color.

A case study of a ten-year-old whose destructive and antisocial behavior toward neighbors results in his incarceration in a children's treatment center. Legal and emotional struggle between the family lawyer who wants the boy to go to a country rehabilitation farm, the child's mother who wants to keep him at home, and the judge who is troubled by the lack of constructive alternatives. Comments by Robert Coles. Produced by CBS News.

What Are We Doing to Our Children? Part 2—Welfare and the Fatherless Family (CAF) 1973. 15 minutes, color.

A low-income apartment complex is the setting for this film. Problems include lack of recreation and day care facilities, drug abuse, illegitimacy, and inadequate medical care. Comments by Robert Coles. Produced by CBS News.

Things to do

Volunteer or paid work. Seek out practical experience with young children, directing your efforts toward settings in which the families of young children are involved. For example, you could work in a day care center with children *and* help with parent meetings or editing the parents' newsletter.

Visit and observe professionals. Observe a staff member of a social agency or county extension office in action as he or she performs daily tasks.

Take courses about families. Select or find courses that focus on family life, social services, or community development. Try to better understand the role families play in our society.

Read about jobs and interview people. Gather as much information as you can concerning the jobs in which you are interested.

People to talk with

Guidance counselor. A counselor can help you assess your career decision and plan a feasible course of action to prepare for and enter your chosen career.

People working with families. Find someone who *is* involved in a career you think you would like. Ask that person about training, interests, and job satisfaction.

Parents and relatives. Your parents or other close relatives can often help you make realistic educational and financial plans for your career.

---

*Film distributors are coded and immediately follow the name of the film; see Appendix 1 for complete name and address of distributor.

Career Pattern Three

Organize Services for Children and Families

Leadership and organizational duties are the primary responsibilities of men and women who work in careers in pattern three. Thus, while a teacher may reach 20 children in career pattern one, a career pattern three leader might reach 20 teachers who in turn will reach 400 children and their families.

Typical decision survey responses for career pattern three

The following typical responses for persons who work in pattern three careers will be helpful before reading the interviews and descriptions of the careers.

Step One: Why do you want to work with or for young children?

Question	Typical Response
1. Why do you feel early childhood is an important period of life?	*A child's early development should not be left to chance.*
2. Why do you want to take an active role in shaping young children's experiences?	*I want to help provide quality services and programs for children and families.*
3. What do you like about young children?	*Young children are enjoyable to interact with. Children represent our hope for the future, and they deserve a good start in life.*
4. What do you find challenging and stimulating about young children?	*Designing programs for young children can really affect their whole lives. I like to work with activities and enjoy planning long-term or large-scale experiences for children. I work best with many children, rather than with individuals.*
5. What kinds of contact do you enjoy with children and adults?	*I enjoy working with and am most comfortable relating to other adults. I sometimes appreciate short periods of direct contact with children.*
6. How do you communicate most comfortably and effectively with children and adults?	*I can explain my ideas and actions to other adults. I lead as much by example as by word.*
7. When you work hard on something, how often or how quickly do you need to see results?	*I know that to get results in a complex situation with many people and ideas, it is necessary for many small changes to merge to form a big change.*
8. What kinds of help and support do you need to continue working on something over a period of time?	*I need to feel that those I work with have confidence in me and trust my judgment. I can plan and execute details and activities without visible success if I am in an accepting atmosphere.*
9. What kind and how much responsibility are you comfortable in assuming?	*I am comfortable assuming full responsibility for program and staff. I can substitute for anyone I supervise because I know the task requirements of my program so well.*

10. To what extent are you confident about explaining the things you do to others who evaluate you?

I recognize that I must be able to justify my actions to the public and to advisory groups that may have little concrete knowledge of my situation.

11. What sort of things that you do leave you with a good feeling about yourself?

I am really pleased when I have been able to direct the efforts of others toward a common goal. I enjoy helping others grow professionally and personally.

12. What kind of image do you want others to have of you?

I want others to see me as a leader who can get things done.

Step Two: What are your skills and abilities?

13. What is your educational background?

Grade School	
High School	
Associate Degree	
Specialized Training or Certificate	
Bachelor's Degree	x
Master's Degree	x
Doctorate	x
Other	x

14. What specific experience have you had related to careers with young children?

Individuals in pattern three typically have considerable experience working with children. They generally have moved into positions of administrative responsibility and thus less frequent contact with children. Some individuals in pattern three have had experience in administration in settings in which young children were not involved.

15. What general abilities have you demonstrated in your experiences with young children?

I can relate well to young children. I can manage individual and group activities as well as develop and implement total programs for children and their families.

16. What abilities have you demonstrated in professional and social experiences with adults?

Others look to me for ideas and guidance. My decisions and judgment are generally respected by others. I can help people set objectives for themselves, assist them in selecting training activities, and give constructive feedback to others about their skills.

17. What abilities have you demonstrated in your experiences with groups and organizations?

I can take charge of events and activities. I can help individuals work together to express their points of view, then set and reach a goal.

18. What initiative abilities have you demonstrated?

I enjoy setting long-range objectives and rarely do things haphazardly. I have developed my own style of management and supervision.

Step Three: What degree of involvement with children is best for you?

Career Pattern	Jobs
1	
2	
3. Jobs that involve directing and organizing programs and services for children and families.	Day care director, Head Start director, school principal, college teacher, public school supervisor, in-service training specialist, home economics teacher, consultant, program coordinator, lab school director, recreation director, school superintendent.

Meet the day care center director

Marian is the director of one of eight day care centers and a network of family day care homes operated by a countywide day care council. This council receives funds through Title XX of the Social Security Act and serves only those clients who are eligible according to state and federal regulations. Marian's center serves approximately 50 children. There is a staff of two cooks, one housekeeper, two group supervisors (similar to head teachers) and six child care workers. The center is open from 6:30 a.m. until 6:30 p.m., and one of Marian's major responsibilities is to make sure that an adequate number of staff members are present throughout the day. Marian must be sure that schedules are worked out well in advance, substitutes are located for employees who are ill, and employee holidays and vacations are taken into account.

How did she come to be a day care center director? Marian has a bachelor's degree in elementary education and taught first grade for several years before she married and had two children of her own. During her children's infancy and early years, she continued as a frequent substitute teacher in the local public schools. While employed as a Head Start teacher, she attended many valuable regional Head Start training workshops. She then moved to a job as director of a day care

The day care center is a lively place, and Marian has frequent informal contacts with the children, even though her major responsibilities are administrative.

center and eventually into the directorship of the day care center where she is now employed. She also worked as a Head Start staff training coordinator and as a parent trainer.

Marian is responsible for the overall planning of the educational program at the day care center and feels that a good working knowledge of children's development and appropriate programming practices is essential. The center is a lively place, and she has frequent informal contacts with the children, even though her major responsibilities are administrative. Occasionally she substitutes for an absent staff member in direct contact with children.

Marian's job involves a great deal of paper work. She completes numerous forms and helps prepare proposals and reports to funding agencies. She keeps records on the children's health and progress, collects fees from parents and does some bookkeeping, keeps attendance records (this is especially important since reimbursement is based on the number of children in attendance), and orders supplies. She also arranges for transportation for children's trips, sets up the center operating schedule, consults with the cooks on menus, and orders food.

Marian is responsible for hiring the staff for her center. Working within the broad policy guidelines of the council, she must interview and employ qualified applicants and then supervise their work. It is important to be sure that all staff can work together as a team and that each is competent. Marian says that this aspect—the hiring and firing of staff—is the most troublesome for her. "I was really not well prepared for handling the supervision of other adults. Sometimes a person can look so good on paper and come off well in an interview, but the first few days on the job and you know it's going to be difficult to help them improve their skills with children and with other staff members. I feel very inadequate in these situations."

In some locations day care is not well accepted, and Marian often finds herself doing public relations work in the community. A related part of her job is work at state and national levels on task forces and with professional organizations. She indicated that a working knowledge of the political process and some basic skills in diplomacy are assets.

Even though Marian has a bachelor's degree in education, she is not required to have such a high level of training in order to function as a day care director in her state. Regulations for qualifications for director vary widely from state to state. She is pleased she has a background in education but knows of other directors who function well without the same experience in teaching young children. Administrative skills are essential, she said. "Above all, you've got to understand that this job involves much, much more than loving children." Salaries vary considerably, too.

The director of a day care center has a great deal of paper work.

Some days Marian finds herself functioning almost as a social worker. This happens when one of her families is experiencing some sort of crisis. She could be the first one to know that a mother has just lost her job, for example. She might then set up appointments with other agencies to assist the mother in handling her problem.

Marian sees her job as day care center director as being very similar in responsibilities to that of a public school principal, although there are vast differences in the training required for each job. Public school principals must hold teaching certificates, have some years of teaching experience, and must complete advanced graduate courses that will contribute to their competence on the job. Day care directors are not required to hold any special licenses or certificates in most states and must meet only minimal requirements of education and experience to hold their jobs.

Marian meets with parent groups in the evening. Sometimes she must travel to other parts of the state for meetings, and sometimes it is necessary to spend evening hours in the office to catch up on paperwork. Marian enjoys her administrative responsibility and finds it challenging to keep all the various aspects of her job running smoothly. Her husband understands her commitment to day care, and his support and help with their children are essential.

It is important to be sure that all staff of the day care center work together as a team and that each is competent.

Look for these men and women organizing services for children and families

College, university, community college, and vocational school teachers

College, university, community college, and vocational school teachers in early childhood education train future and current teachers. Slightly more than one-half of them instruct undergraduates; another one-third teach both graduates and undergraduates; and about one-tenth work only with graduate students. Most teachers lecture and conduct classroom discussions; some provide individual instruction or supervise independent study. College teachers must keep up

Most college teachers lecture and conduct classroom discussions; some provide individual instruction or supervise independent study.

with developments in their field by reading and publishing current material, participating in professional activities, and conducting research. The importance of research and publication varies from one institutional level to another. The interview in career pattern four with a university-based researcher (p. 49) describes the career of a college teacher for whom research is of primary interest. In addition to time spent on preparation, instruction, and evaluation, college and university teachers participate in faculty activities; work with student organizations; work with the college administration; and in other ways serve the institution and the community. Some are department heads and supervise other faculty members and degree programs.

A master's degree is usually required for an initial appointment as instructor. For advancement to higher ranks, research, publication, and work experience in the field are necessary. The employment outlook is not very favorable because of the increase in the number of graduates of master's and doctoral programs and the drop in college enrollments. College and university teachers usually work long hours every week, but may have a nine or ten month contract. Scheduled class sessions, committee meetings, supervision, and training sessions for students in the field are supplemented with many more hours spent in preparation, reading, and writing of articles, reports, grant proposals, books, etc. Faculty give generously of their time to students for counseling, course help, and activity advising. Briefcases loaded with work are the norm most nights and weekends.

Most college teachers in the field of education are involved in teacher training through teaching "methods" courses, supervising student teachers, and/or advising prospective teachers. Teacher training requires extensive knowledge of the skills and personal attributes required of a good teacher and the ability to transmit this knowledge to students. Those involved in teacher training need to be good judges of individual potential. They must also be tactful, understanding, and able to make their expectations clear to students.

Faculty working in education departments may teach a number of general early childhood education courses on topics such as play, program design, observation of young children, and methods and materials for young children's programs. Sometimes faculty will specialize in particular content areas such as language arts, science, or math. Faculty in departments other than education may specialize in areas related to young children and form a loose campuswide network of interdisciplinary focus on young children and their families. Psychology, sociology, rural sociology, agriculture, law, architecture, nursing, human development, nutrition, and speech are a few examples of disciplines where individual scholars may apply their knowledge to young children.

Faculty members have the opportunity to make a major impact on the future shape of children's programming and professional practices. They can

initiate changes in training techniques and respond to changing needs in the field. An example is the growing response to the need for formal training for people who work in day care settings. In addition, many early childhood faculty have strongly supported increased training experiences to prepare individuals to work with young handicapped children.

Principals, supervisors, coordinators, and directors

These individuals manage, supervise, and administer school or early childhood education programs. Broadly considered, their jobs are human and public relations, since they must be able to hold up well under stress and resolve conflicts. These people must be able to see the comprehensive view while dealing with details, be diplomatic and tactful, and should like to work with people.

The requirements for certification as a principal or supervisor of an early childhood program vary from state to state. In general, some classroom experience is necessary, and many states require a master's degree in administration for principals. Salaries are usually higher than those for classroom teachers with the same fringe benefits. The employment outlook is fair. A principal who seeks advancement may need to specialize in some area of administration.

Principals and other similar workers must know and respect the community the school serves; the interests, problems, and goals of the people; their

Although their primary responsibility is managing teachers and staff, principals should have contact with students and must be able to work with them effectively.

Career Pattern Three

educational and ethnic backgrounds; and personal and material resources. Relationships with the teachers are of prime importance since the attitudes and morale of the staff are shaped largely by the kind of leadership provided. These individuals visit and observe classes in session, make suggestions, and evaluate the work of each teacher. They also supervise the work of all program or school employees such as secretaries, custodians, etc. Although their primary responsibility is managing teachers and staff, principals should have contact with students and must be able to work with them effectively.

Because of their leadership position and authority, principals and supervisors can have a direct impact on programming practices for young children within schools under their jurisdiction. Through sensitive supervision, persuasive demonstration of techniques, and constructive criticism and praise, they can shape teachers' practices. Establishing philosophical guidelines for programs and monitoring daily practices to encourage consistency between philosophy and practice are necessary components of their jobs. Knowledge about curriculum, current educational practice, and current research are a critical basis for developing and implementing this philosophy.

Principals and supervisors set the tone for early childhood programs. Through sharing of experiences among teachers, provision of materials and information, and support of teachers' ideas, they can help establish clear channels of communication and strong internal program support. Responsibility for creating and maintaining a challenging, stimulating working environment tuned to developments in the field of early education rests primarily with the principal or other supervisor.

Home economics/family living teachers

Home economics teachers in junior high and high schools usually teach courses in nutrition, child development, marriage and family, and basic homemaking skills such as sewing and cooking. Schools may provide fully-equipped demonstration kitchens, rooms furnished in a homelike manner, and fully-equipped preschool programs. Home economics courses may be electives or may provide advanced vocational training for jobs after high

school. Recently, considerable emphasis has been placed on preparing young people for future marriage and parenthood, and courses dealing with these topics are likely to be taken by large numbers of students.

Home economics teachers must have bachelor's degrees in home economics and have completed the courses required for teacher certification. They receive the same salaries as other teachers. The employment outlook is not optimistic at present.

Home economics teachers handle varying loads of courses. Classes in skills such as sewing and cooking are likely to be long periods involving materials preparation and demonstration. Family and marriage topics may involve considerable lecture preparation, recruiting of guest speakers, arranging for simulated exercises in problem resolution, and in-class moderating of discussions and student comments. Laboratory programs for young children may operate for several weeks each school term, during which time the home economics teacher serves as head teacher for the young children attending the program as well as an instructor for the high school students. With student help, the home economics teacher will recruit children, plan and run the program, work with parents of the children, and help students relate experiences in the program to developmental information about young children. Thus, home economics teachers are included in this career pattern.

Home economics teachers must be skilled group discussion leaders and must be sensitive to the developmental needs of their teenage students while encouraging exploration of early childhood development and feelings about young children. Junior high and high school students are only recently removed from their own childhoods, and this may be an ideal time to explore their attitudes and reactions to young children. Working effectively with young people requires a sensitive approach that encourages their growth toward maturity.

In-service training specialists

In-service specialists develop programs for professionals and paraprofessionals working directly with children and families in a number of different settings. Basically, an in-service specialist works with people in their job settings,

In-service specialists strive for a balance between presenting new information, stretching individuals to grow and change, and encouraging staff to feel confident and competent on the job.

fitting the timing and content of training to current needs. Training may take place in a local program with only a small group, on a regional or agency basis, or on a college campus in sessions over a period of time with participants coming from unrelated programs. In-service training may give college credit, certificates of participation, or no formal recognition other than personal benefits.

The in-service specialist must be familiar with the setting in which participants work, perhaps having worked in similar jobs at one time. Specialists generally have a master's or higher degree and are associated with an institution of higher learning or an agency. In-service programs take place at the convenience of participants, sometimes in the evening, on weekends, or in late afternoon after children have left for the day.

An in-service specialist needs to be knowledgeable in curriculum development, child development, psychology, curriculum materials, and other areas relating to teaching. He or she must have group management skills necessary to work effectively with adults.

One frequently requested topic for in-service training is discipline. The following example illustrates how an in-service specialist might pursue planning and giving a three-hour workshop on a Friday afternoon for the staff of the local program. No formal credit will be given, attendance will be required, and the specialist will be paid a flat fee plus travel expenses and reimbursement for any consumable materials.

Before the session the specialist may visit the program to talk with staff, observe staff interactions with children, and collect information about the specific needs of the staff. Such a visit is not always feasible, and the in-service specialist may need to rely on the director's assessment of the situation. Preparation for the session may take up to ten hours and include preparing handouts and discussion sheets, writing directions for role-play sessions on resolving problems, and locating any audiovisual equipment needed.

The session involves a carefully orchestrated sequence of discussion, information presentation, participant activity, and assignment completion. Friday afternoon, or any period after a long work day, is not the easiest time to generate enthusiasm for learning, even on a topic of such immediate interest as discipline. Specialists frequently come prepared with alternative plans for session activities and materials. It is not unusual to discover upon arrival that basic information on child development is needed before any fruitful exploration of discipline strategies can occur. Other times it will be obvious that opposing points of view exist, and the specialist may need to serve as mediator to help the group accept its differences and reconcile them if possible. Ten hours of carefully planned activities can be quickly shelved in such situations.

In-service training is a challenging activity, demanding in professional expertise, personal diplomacy, tact, and leadership. The opportunity for significant impact on the daily experiences of children is great, since in-service specialists work closely with the staffs of programs. In-service specialists strive for a balance between presenting new information, stretching individuals to grow and change in desired directions while supporting existing practice, and encouraging staff to feel confident and competent on the job. Evaluating what participants learned and determining whether they practice new skills are valuable in planning future sessions.

Other supervisory careers

Many other positions exist that require supervision of programs: psychological services, nursing or homemaker services, school superintendents, recreation program directors, and consulting firms to industry regarding provision of quality child care facilities, for example.

Qualifications, salaries, and job opportunities vary widely, but individuals usually enter these fields after having first gained experience in working with children or families. Each involves supervision or training of other adults who will in turn work directly with families and/or children.

Where do you stand?

As you have done with each previous career pattern, review your responses on the Decision Survey for completeness, then compare and rank your responses with those that are typical for this career pattern (pp. 38-39). Enter your ratings on the Rating Sheet before beginning "Career Pattern Four."

Resources

Almy, M. *The Early Childhood Educator at Work.* New York: McGraw-Hill, 1975.

Concerned with a new professional role for the early childhood educator. The first half describes several programs and examines the field of early childhood education. The second half deals more directly with the role of the early childhood educator in teaching, in research, and in working with teachers and other adults.

Becker, C. *Career Development Guides: Child Development.* University City, Mo.: University City School District, 1974. (ERIC Document Reproduction Service #ED 106 633.)

A course outline and sample unit plans for a one semester, secondary school child development course geared toward career development.

Brottman, M. A. "Preschool-Primary Teachers for Inner-City Schools." *The Elementary School Journal,* 60, no. 7, April 1969, pp. 352-358.

Preschool and elementary school functions could be coordinated through teachers who are prepared to teach children from three to eight years of age.

Brunner, C. "Staff Development Activities for Aides." In *Aides to Teachers and Children,* ed. S. Sunderlin. Washington, D.C.: Association for Childhood Education International, 1968.

Basic ingredients of a successful aide program are dealt with.

Butler, A. L. *Early Childhood Education: Planning and Administering Programs.* New York: D. Van Nostrand Co., 1974.

Chapter 3 discusses the role of school administrators, teachers, social workers, health and nutrition personnel, and teacher aides. Staff training and selection are also covered.

Career Planning and Progression for a Child Development Center. Washington, D.C.: Child Development Services Bureau, 1973. (ERIC Document Reproduction Service #ED 086 308.)

Describes a plan for the development and advancement of Head Start program assistants through a sequence of career progression steps.

Chambers, G. S. "Staff Selection and Training." In *Day Care: Resources for Decision,* ed. E. H. Grotberg. Washington, D.C.: Office of Economic Opportunity, n.d.

A variety of innovative approaches to effectively guarantee the paraprofessional ongoing education for career advancement are described.

Child Care Job Training Curriculum. Columbia, S.C.: Clemson University, 1973. (ERIC Document Reproduction Service #ED 090 412.)

High school program designed for home economics classes. Part One provides an orientation to child care employment. Part Two focuses on the specific job skills necessary for work as a child care aide.

Career Pattern Three

Cohen, M.; Gordon, E.; and Krivin, J. "Student Teachers Look at Student Teaching." In *That All Children May Learn We Must Learn: Looking Forward to Teaching*, ed. M. Cohen. Washington, D.C.: Association for Childhood Education International, 1971.

Examination of many of the problems faced by student teachers and their suggested solutions; full of implications for teacher trainers, supervising teachers, and potential student teachers.

Croft, D. *Be Honest with Yourself*. Belmont, Calif.: Wadsworth, 1976.

Incidents are provided for self-evaluation by teachers and child care workers in training to analyze their commitment to working with young children.

De Orio, R., and Anderson, M. J. "Junior High School Students and Young Children." *Young Children* 29, no. 4 (May 1974): 214-217.

Junior high school students involved in a nursery school classroom as part of a study of child development.

Ferguson, G. E., et al. *Family Living, Personal Culture, Child Development, and Careers in Home Economics. Career Development Project*. University City, Mo.: University City School District, 1972. (ERIC Document Reproduction Service #ED 107 784.)

Four instructional units in home economics designed for the seventh through ninth grades.

Flynn, J. "College Training for Head Start Workers." *Children* 17, no. 2 (March-April 1970): 49-52.

The Head Start Supplementary Training Program is described in detail.

Howe, A. "Teacher's Aide or Teacher's Maid." *Early Years*, February 1972, pp. 52-56.

Describes a training program for teacher's aides in early education classrooms.

Jacob, S., ed. *Manual on Organization, Financing, and Administration of Day Care Centers in New York City*. 2nd ed. New York: Bank Street College of Education, 1971. (ERIC Document Reproduction Service #ED 058 967.)

How to start a day care center in New York City, with information on the agencies involved, financing through various sources, staffing a center, legal matters, planning a health program, equipment, etc.

Jordan, D. C. "Early Childhood Education—It's a Science." In *Early Childhood Education: It's an Art? It's a Science?* ed. J. D. Andrews. Washington, D.C.: National Association for the Education of Young Children, 1976.

The Anisa Model is an attempt to establish a comprehensive educational system built on scientific foundations. This article deals with the need for such a system; the first principles and the value of the Anisa theory.

Katz, L. G. "Developmental Stages of Preschool Teachers." *Elementary School Journal* 73, no. 1 (October 1972): 50-54.

The developmental stages are: survival, consolidation, renewal, and maturity. Implications these stages have for teacher training are discussed.

Kysilka, M. L. "The University's Role in the Preservice Education of Teachers." *Educational Leadership* 30, no. 5 (February 1973): 425-427.

Three common complaints about teacher education are dealt with and some solutions are suggested.

Lehane, S., and Goldman, R. *Building the Steps of the Career Ladder*. Kent, Ohio: Kent State University, 1975. (ERIC Document Reproduction Service #ED 114 190.)

Describes an experimental bachelor of arts program designed to meet the special needs of experienced early childhood workers who have minimal exposure to higher education.

Lowe, A. "Becoming a Teacher." In *That All Children May Learn We Must Learn: Looking Forward to Teaching*, ed. M. Cohen. Washington, D.C.: Association for Childhood Education International, 1971.

Overview of the direct experience component in teacher education programs.

McKenna, A. *Training Preschool Personnel*. Irish Committee of OMEP, World Organization for Early Childhood Education, Paris, France.

Describes various types of preschool programs; the need for day care facilities and personnel; the training of preschool personnel; and recommendations for improving training procedures.

Morris, M. S. "The California Credential Story: A New Specialization for Teachers of Young Children." *Young Children* 25, no. 5 (May 1970): 268-281.

California established a Standard Teaching Credential in 1969 with Specialization in Early Childhood Teaching. This article discusses the history of the law and its implications for early childhood education.

Murphy, L. B. "Multiple Factors in Learning in the Day Care Center." in *A Lap to Sit on . . . and Much More: Helps for Day Care Workers 1*, ed. M. Cohen. Washington, D.C.: Association for Childhood Education International, 1971.

The director's role in a day care center is described.

Parten, C. B. "A Training Program for Volunteers." *Young Children* 26, no. 1 (October 1970): 27-33.

This six-week training program involved the training of mothers and grandmothers in the barrios of Los Angeles through the Council of Mexican-American Affairs Head Start. They were prepared to work directly with children in the classroom and to use these techniques in the home.

Peterson, M. *Application of Vocational Development Theory to Career Education*. Information series no. 80. Columbus, Ohio: Ohio State University, July 1973. (ERIC Document Reproduction Service #ED 090 393.)

Five vocational development theories are presented to show how they can be applied in career education programs.

Pope, L. and Crump, R. "School Drop-Outs as Assistant Teachers." *Young Children*, 21, no. 1 (October 1965): 13-23.

Describes a successful program where school drop-outs were trained as teacher aides.

Rose, I. B., and White, M. E. *Child Care and Development Occupations: Competency Based Teaching Modules*. Washington, D.C.: U. S. Government Printing Office, 1974.

"Overview for Program Development"

Gives the rationale behind competency based teaching modules.

Module 1: "Child Care and Development Occupations"

Purpose is to develop an understanding of child care/development services and occupations. The appendixes include job descriptions and task analysis for child care/development occupations.

Module 20: "Program Planning"

Trainees are given an understanding of the need for planning and scheduling in programs for the preschool child and of the need for establishing program goals.

Module 23: "Administration and Supervision"

Skills necessary to become a good administrator and supervisor: setting up child care programs, personnel management, business practices, public relations techniques, evaluation, human relations, employer-employee relationships, and self-improvement.

Spodek, B. "Constructing a Model for a Teacher Education Program in Early Childhood Education." *Contemporary Education* 40 (1969): 145-149.

Suggests a new approach to teacher education; describes the assumptions that the program is based on and the components of the program. Emphasis is on relevancy and flexibility.

Spodek, B. "Staff Requirements in Early Childhood Education." In *Seventy-First Yearbook of the National Society for the Study of Education, Part II,* ed. I. J. Gordon. Chicago: University of Chicago Press, 1972.

Staffing arrangements and the roles of teachers, administrators, supervisors, aides, and volunteers are discussed. Certification requirements and training programs are also dealt with.

Spodek, B., ed. *Teacher Education: Of the Teacher, by the Teacher, for the Child.* Washington, D.C.: National Association for the Education of Young Children, 1974.

Contains articles on various approaches to teacher education and the issues that need to be considered.

Stevens, J. H., Jr., and King, E. W. *Administering Early Childhood Education Programs.* Boston: Little, Brown & Co., 1976.

Deals with the broader issues of early childhood education and how programs serving young children should function. Is not a "how-to" book.

Teacher Guide for Business, Education, Child Services, Health Services, Construction Technology (Grades 7-12). Pleasant Hill, Oreg.: Pleasant Hill School District, September 1973. (ERIC Document Reproduction Service #ED 118 745.)

Program descriptions for each occupational cluster are provided. Resource lists (books, pamphlets, and audiovisual aids) are included.

Zaccaria, M. A., et al. *Texas Day Care Study. Final Report: Occupational Analysis of Day Care Personnel.* San Antonio, Tex.: University of Texas, February 1976. (ERIC Document Reproduction Service #ED 122 939.)

Describes the results of a study involving the development, administration, and analysis of a job inventory of Texas day care positions.

Films*

Diagnosing Group Operations (IU) 1963. 30 minutes.

This film is helpful for those who work on teams. It includes causes of conflict in groups and how to identify symptoms. From the Dynamics of Leadership series. Produced by NET.

Impact of a Teacher's Behavior on Learners and Learning—John Withall (PSU) 1969. 71 minutes. #PCR-2197.

An unrehearsed teaching demonstration for inservice and preservice teachers. Two instructional modes emphasize the teacher's verbal and nonverbal behavior on learners. Guidelines for systematic analysis of teaching behavior are presented. Teachers' self-evaluations and discussion are stimulated.

The Learning Society (AAHE) 1973. 20 minutes, color.

Presents information about forms of nontraditional study, where practical knowledge and life experience are applied to academic credit. Use of television and other media, individualized and small-group instruction are described.

A Man's Reach (OSU) 1964. 35 minutes.

A day in the life of a school superintendent. The complex, demanding nature of the job and the relationship of the superintendent to the school system are highlighted.

Things to do

Volunteer or paid work. Seek out practical experience with young children. Choose settings in which you work directly with someone who organizes and administers the program or service.

Visit and observe professionals. Try to observe a leader in action. Talk to someone who works for that person. Try to get a feel for the extent and complexity of his or her many job responsibilities.

Develop and exercise leadership skills. Participate in and lead groups. Try to improve and refine your leadership abilities.

Read about jobs and interview people. Gather as much information as you can concerning the jobs in which you are interested.

People to talk with

Guidance counselor. A counselor can help you assess your career decision and plan a feasible course of action to prepare for and enter your chosen career.

People working in leadership roles with children and families. Find someone who *is* involved in a career you think you would like. Ask that person about their training, interests, and job satisfactions.

Parents and relatives. Your parents or other close relatives can often help you make realistic educational and financial plans for your career.

*Film distributors are coded and immediately follow the name of the film; see Appendix 1 for complete name and address of distributor.

Career Pattern Four

Provide Information to Professionals Who Work with Children and Families

Career pattern four includes individuals who are experts in various content areas related to programs and services for children and families. These men and women provide support services and disseminate their information and skills to other professionals who work with children, families, agencies, services, and programs that more directly affect young children. These individuals are not likely to be found in frequent or sustained contact directly with children or families, and they do not usually supervise others or administer programs.

Careers in this cluster include a wide range of professional interests. The most common jobs are university-based researchers, school psychologists, instructional technologists, librarians, teacher resource center staff, and agency and referral specialists. As you might expect, individuals who choose these careers are typically highly trained.

Career pattern four people exemplify a strong orientation toward skills and knowledge in particular content areas. Many individuals who successfully pursue these careers have worked at one time or another directly with young children. Such experience often aids them in providing realistic and practical help to those they serve.

Typical decision survey responses for career pattern four

You will find it extremely helpful to review these typical responses to the Decision Survey before reading the interviews and descriptions of the careers that follow.

Step One: Why do you want to work with or for young children?

Question	Typical Response
1. Why do you feel early childhood is an important period of life?	*The early years provide the foundation for later life and learning.*
2. Why do you want to take an active role in shaping young children's experiences?	*It is important to understand the processes and conditions of early growth and development. Accurate, basic information regarding these processes is essential for all who work with young children.*
3. What do you like about young children?	*I enjoy meeting and interacting with children, but I prefer not to spend a lot of time with them.*
4. What do you find challenging and stimulating about young children?	*It is fascinating to explore the process of children's development. It helps me understand and appreciate the complexities of human behavior.*
5. What kinds of contact do you enjoy with children and adults?	*I like having brief contacts with a number of children and observing them in their activities. Primarily, I enjoy working with other adults.*
6. How do you communicate most comfortably and effectively with children and adults?	*I'm effective in speaking to groups of people and often prepare written reports based on my work.*
7. When you work hard on something, how often or how quickly do you need to see results?	*I can disseminate information very quickly to other professionals, but I often do not know what impact my work has had. I can work for long periods of time without any substantive feedback.*
8. What kinds of help and support do you need to continue working on something over a period of time?	*I generally know if I am doing a good job, but I appreciate feedback from colleagues and peers on my written reports, materials, and speeches.*

9. What kind and how much responsibility are you comfortable in assuming?

I like being self-directed and being able to assume as much responsibility as I want related to helping provide others with the information they need to work effectively.

10. To what extent are you confident about explaining the things you do to others who evaluate you?

I understand that my work must meet standards established by my professional colleagues. My work speaks for itself.

11. What sort of things that you do leave you with a good feeling about yourself?

Completing a project successfully and finding answers to questions is important. Getting a paper or article published is rewarding. Speeches I give that stimulate thinking help me know how my work affects others.

12. What kind of image do you want others to have of you?

I want others to think of me as knowledgeable and competent in my field. I want them to think I have had an influence on the way they interact with children.

Step Two: What are your skills and abilities?

13. What is your educational background?

Grade School	
High School	
Associate Degree	
Specialized Training or Certificate	
Bachelor's Degree	
Master's Degree	X
Doctorate	X
Other	

14. What specific experiences have you had related to careers with young children?

Individuals gain experiences in scholarly activities including research, teaching, and service through graduate training. Many have extensive experience working with young children and/or families and as teachers and program leaders. Such experience usually precedes graduate training.

15. What general abilities have you demonstrated in your experiences with young children?

I am good at observing small details of children's behavior. I can often put these together to identify patterns of development, then relate these to abstract concepts, to theoretical constructs, and build systems to be tested.

16. What abilities have you demonstrated in professional and social experiences with adults?

I can easily change styles of interacting with adults: listening, guiding, leading, directing, supervising, chatting, etc.

17. What abilities have you demonstrated in your experiences with groups and organizations?

I often lead groups through my ideas and suggestions. I am a poised, polished speaker, comfortable in public settings.

Question	Typical Response
18. What initiative abilities have you demonstrated?	*I can identify problems or issues that interest me and pursue them diligently by myself. My own ideas keep me going much of the time. I like to locate and share curriculum and research resources. It is valuable to me to be up to date with information in the field. I enjoy helping others define their problems and identify possible resources for investigation and resolution.*

Step Three: What degree of involvement with children is best for you?

Career Pattern	Jobs
1	
2	
3	
4. Jobs that involve working with other professionals who in turn work with children and families.	Researcher, evaluation specialist, instructional technologist, agency specialist, school psychologist, librarian, teacher resource center staff member, author/editor.

Meet the researcher who investigates problems in child development and early childhood education

Steve is expected to continually write proposals to get grants from sources outside the university to support his research.

Most people who devote their professional time and energy to research activities are employed by universities, private research companies, research offices supported by private foundations, or by the federal government. Numerous federal agencies such as the Administration for Children, Youth and Families, the Office of Education, the National Institute of Mental Health, and the National Institute of Child Health and Human Development, all based in Washington, D.C., employ educational researchers. Private corporations such as Educational Testing Service and Science Research Associates also have large staffs of educational and psychological researchers.

To catch a glimpse of the life of a researcher who is interested in looking at problems involving children, their education, and family living, we talked with Steve, who is employed as a faculty member at a large university. The terms of his contract are such that he is expected to continually write proposals to get extra monies (grants) from sources

outside the university to support his research interests. When he has many such projects under way, he does not do much teaching or engage in other activities typical of a faculty member; he works almost all the time on his research contracts.

How did he happen to choose research as a career? Steve grew up in a suburban part of a large midwestern city. As a teenager, he held part-time jobs as a delivery boy for a florist, as a dishwasher, and as a drug store clerk. There was no question that he would go to college, and he entered as a commercial airline pilot major and spent several enjoyable college years flying. As part of a required course in psychology, he came into contact with

a professor who had the students engage in brief psychological experiments. Steve was assigned to an experiment that involved teaching blind people mobility skills. He was hooked on research from that moment.

The professor encouraged him to change to a psychology major, which he eventually did, and after completing a bachelor's degree, Steve continued as a graduate student in psychology. He worked as a research assistant for the same professor and continued to perfect his skills in research design (planning experiments) and statistics. He was part of a team of research assistants working on the same type of research projects, and there was a great spirit of camaraderie among them as they spent long hours waiting for a printout at the computer center or collaborating to write up the results of their experiments. Ten years later, Steve remembers, "We were all so poor as graduate students that we would have to save for months to have even a small party, but we all knew there would be better times. I guess the fact that we were all in there together working long hours, rushing to finish projects on time, and still getting good grades in our own graduate work made it easier to take. Most of us had a pretty strong sense of humor, and it sure helped when things got especially hectic on a proposal or when we were winding up a project."

Upon completion of a master's degree in psychology, Steve took a job with a commercial test publisher as a

A team of graduate students assists Steve with various aspects of his projects.

researcher. He was responsible for conducting field studies of new tests, which involved much cooperative work with people in other departments in the company.

At first the responsibilities of the job as well as the salary were enough to sustain Steve's interest, but eventually the business of conducting similar research studies over and over became routine and somewhat boring.

Steve had maintained some of his friendships from his graduate student days and was interested to learn about the doctoral program in child development one of his friends was in when they chanced to meet at a convention a few years later. Since he had not been thinking too seriously about going back to graduate school, Steve's reserve finances were low; and he

thought long and hard about what he wanted to do with the rest of his life and about his family responsibilities. He did return to graduate school and eventually completed a doctoral degree in child development and early education. His special area of interest, and the area in which he still concentrates most of his research, is children's language development.

Steve has been employed by a university department of child development for several years. He has continued his strong interest in research and spends most of his time functioning as a researcher. What is his life like day to day? He travels frequently to Washington, D.C., in order to keep in touch with priorities of the various government funding agencies that might support his work. He is also expected to travel to professional meetings and seminars to report on his research to other professionals. There is constant activity in his office. He has a team of graduate student assistants to help with the various aspects of his projects. Steve spends a considerable amount of time counseling these budding professionals about their own careers and helps them begin their own research programs.

As deadlines for new proposals or for completion of projects approach, the pace of activity becomes hectic. Steve recalls that on several occasions the

graduate students, secretaries, research colleagues, and spouses were required to help collate a final report. The real excitement comes when the computer printout is studied, however. The statistical techniques that are used to analyze the information gathered in the research study are now ready for inspection; and the idea is either supported, or the results prove to be inconclusive. There is always the possibility that a significant contribution to knowledge in the field will result from one of Steve's experiments. While Steve has contributed much information to the field, he has little interest in translating his research findings into practical classroom applications. Other university faculty members (such as those described in career pattern three) make important contributions in the translation of theory into practice.

Life is hardly ever slow and quiet for Steve. He likes it that way. He may spend long hours reading or thinking about a problem, and this is physically exhausting work. At other times his travel schedule is heavy, or there are project deadlines to meet, and efforts among the project team members must be coordinated. He has to be a manager as well as a thinker, and above all he has to have a strong knowledge background in his specialty and in the techniques of research design and statistics.

The real excitement comes when the computer printout with the research results is studied.

Look for these men and women who provide information to professionals who work with children and families

Consultants: early childhood education, evaluation, and curriculum specialists

Consultants are hired by an organization for a limited period of time to bring in expertise unavailable within the existing staff. A consultant usually has extensive experience in the field of early childhood education and an advanced degree, often a doctorate. Program evaluation specialists need basic skills in evaluation techniques and research methodology; sometimes experience in the type of program being evaluated is required. A curriculum specialist is often required to have experience in classroom instruction.

Consultants are hired on a project-by-project basis. They may be self-employed or work for a consulting firm. While working on a project, the time demands and pressures are considerable. However, there may be periods of unemployment between jobs.

During a project, a consultant may help design a program, evaluate a program or a program component, design materials, train staff, or provide case-by-case advice on students. He or she assists others in solving their problems through a willingness to listen and by helping them further specify their goals, objectives, and problems. This requires skills in facilitating group work and in bringing out hidden agendas and motivations. A consultant must be able to translate theory into practice and be able to communicate clearly both in writing and verbally. An important part of consulting is the organization of data; recommendations are then based on the available data.

By helping to improve the quality of the programs that serve young children, consultants meet an important need. Consulting is a highly competitive field, and the employment outlook is dependent upon the amount of money available for special projects. Salaries vary, depending on the number of consulting jobs one is able to contract. Often the consultants must engage in marketing their services while they are at work on other projects.

Author/editor

An author or editor of professional journals and books usually conducts research, confers with others in early childhood education or child development, and writes or edits manuscripts for publication. Two fundamental requirements of this field are training in the art of writing and graphics communication, and knowledge of early childhood education and child development. A bachelor's degree is usually necessary.

Authors or editors may freelance or may be employed by a specific journal (usually published by educational associations) or a publishing company. People often enter this field after having taught, conducted research, or worked in some other capacity with young children. Long hours of work under extreme pressure may be necessary to meet deadlines. Some professional journals have volunteer editors with full-time responsibilities as teachers or program administrators who do journal editing as a professional service.

Along with skills in writing and/or editing, an author or editor needs to present ideas in clear, logical, and accurate form and to recognize the core of a topic along with the significant facts. Interpersonal and public relations skills are also needed since an author or editor works with people as well as ideas.

By keeping others informed of current research and ideas, an author or editor contributes to the expertise of those working with young children. Employment depends on the current state of the field, and salaries cover a wide range.

School psychologists

School psychologists work directly with children (see career pattern one, p. 10), but they also act as consultants to classroom teachers who may be having problems with children. They interpret tests for teachers and help them use the test results effectively. They are often involved in developing individualized programs for handicapped children. Besides a knowledge of psychology, child development, and testing, a good working relationship with administrators and teachers is necessary.

Instructional technologist

Instructional technologists or media specialists use their expertise in theories of instruction and media and materials to assist teachers. They need to have extensive, up-to-date knowledge of the many types of instructional materials and media available and an understanding of the theories of instruction and systems. The field has changed dramatically since the advent of computers. Spurred by computer programmers and technologists, educators have been encouraged to think of instruction as a system with identifiable parts and working relationships. "Systems approaches" theories of instruction have since been developed and are usually strongly embraced by the instructional technologists.

People who hold positions as instructional technologists are specialists in designing and implementing instructional systems. As such, they are knowledgeable in the specification of educational objectives, both short- and long-range, the design of educational

Instructional technologists use their expertise in theories of instruction and media and materials to assist teachers.

Provide Information to Professionals

procedures intended to help learners reach the objectives, and the design of matched evaluation procedures so the effectiveness of the system for the learner can be documented.

These jobs often require evening work and frequent trips to educational meetings and conventions. Because they are in a position to recommend the purchase of large amounts of materials and expensive instructional equipment, instructional technologists are often pressured by sales representatives.

An instructional technologist usually, but not always, comes to the position with a background of teaching experience. In some states, the position requires additional training, and often a specialist certification is needed. This training program is often completed in conjunction with a master's degree, and in some states, courses beyond the master's level are required for certification.

When they are employed by school districts, instructional technologists earn according to their placement on a salary scale based on their advanced degrees and years of experience. In private or government positions, salaries are higher. With the increasing complexity of instructional materials and the expansion in the use of computers, this area should grow.

Specialist in the education of the handicapped

The passage of Public Law 94-142, The Education for All Handicapped Children Act, has increased the demand for those who specialize in various aspects of programming for the handicapped. The provisions of P.L. 94-142 are comprehensive and influence everyone in education, medicine, law, and social services. The law mandates an appropriate education at public expense for all handicapped children, age 5 to 18 years. It also provides monetary incentives for those who sponsor programs for preschool handicapped children, age 3 to 5 years. In states in which educational programs are already available to those in the 3 to 5 year or 18 to 21 year age ranges, these educational services must be extended to the handicapped.

One of the important features of the law for educators is that the educational programs designed for handicapped children must be individually tailored for each child through preparation of an individualized educational program (IEP). The IEP must include information about the child's present performance in relevant areas, long- and short-range objectives, and specific educational procedures and support services that will be required to achieve the goals. The IEP must be developed jointly by teachers (both regular and special educators), professionals (speech therapists, school psychologists, remedial reading teachers, etc.), the child's parents, and the child if possible and appropriate.

This involvement is the basis for the prediction of emerging careers for consultants. No longer will special educators, regular classroom teachers, speech therapists, mobility specialists for the blind, school psychologists, and clinical psychologists operate independently. Special educators are likely to serve as consultants or resource teachers to other teachers, rather than teaching handicapped children in self-contained classrooms. School psychologists are gradually moving toward a new role definition as educational consultants.

In providing this individualized education, handicapped and nonhandicapped children are to be educated together unless the nature of the child's handicap is such that he or she cannot be satisfactorily accommodated in regular classrooms. This provision of P.L. 94-142 is popularly referred to as mainstreaming. The essential idea is not to bring all handicapped children into regular classrooms, but to move each handicapped child into whatever environment is the least restrictive. As handicapped children are moved into these least restrictive environments, those who have not had much contact with them will require help from specialists in integrating these handicapped children into the classroom.

In order to make certain that education is provided to *all* handicapped children, P.L. 94-142 mandates continuing efforts be made to identify children with handicaps. Often, but not exclusively, the "child find" efforts are focused on young children.

Other careers

Libraries, government-funded agencies, information clearinghouses, teacher resource centers, educational television, and professional organizations employ specialists in the above areas as well as many others including: staff development specialists, administrators, and information specialists.

Employment opportunities vary with funding availability, and salaries cover a wide range.

Where do you stand?

As you have done with each previous career pattern, review your responses on the Decision Survey for completeness, then compare and rank your responses with those that are typical for this career pattern (pp. 47-49). Enter your ratings on the Rating Sheet before beginning "Career Pattern Five."

Resources

A Context Analysis of Early Childhood Development. Final Report. Austin, Tex.: Educational Development Corp., April 1973. (ERIC Document Reproduction Service #ED 097 114.)

Examines the present conditions in early childhood education and development.

Buktenica, N. A. "A Multidisciplinary Training Team in the Public Schools." *Journal of School Psychology* 8 (1970): 220-225.

The need to involve a multidisciplinary team in the public schools is described. New roles of some team members are proposed.

Cauman, J. "What Is the Nursery School Team?" In *Nursery School Portfolio.* Washington, D.C.: Association for Childhood Education International, 1969.

Ways of facilitating communication between members and the efficient use of all the members are considered.

Dent, M. W. "Consulting with Teachers Via the Guidance Team." *Personnel and Guidance Journal* 52, no. 10 (1974): 685-688.

Since counselors are trained to understand human behavior, they are in a unique position to foster teamwork and communication within the schools. This article describes the organization of a guidance team to serve in a consultative capacity to teachers.

Endres, M. P., and Lisack, J. P. *Child Day Care in Indiana. Manpower and Training Requirements.* Lafayette, Ind.: Purdue University, July 1972. (ERIC Document Reproduction Service #ED 068 626.)

A survey of child care facilities to standardize occupational titles, duties, responsibilities, and qualifications of four levels of child care specialists; and to provide educational, civic, and government planners with information to assist them in planning educational programs, certification requirements, and policies for child care programs.

Fine, M. J., and Epstein, I. J. "The School Psychologist's Contribution to the Community Mental Health Center." *Journal of School Psychology* 7 (1969): 70-74.

Arguments for involvement of school psychologists in the community mental health center are presented.

Friedman, J., and Hauser, A. L. "Developing a Teacher Resource Center for Preschool Educators." *Young Children* 34, no. 1 (November 1978): 28-32.

Ideas for planning and operating a teacher center with workshops, a supply shop, and libraries.

Lauver, P. J. "Consulting with Teachers: A Systematic Approach." *Personnel and Guidance Journal* 52, no. 8 (1974): 535-540.

Systematic procedures for beginning and sustaining a consulting relationship between school counselors and teachers are presented.

Morgan, L. B. "The Many Faces of a Counselor: A Dialogue." *Personnel and Guidance Journal* 52, no. 10 (1974): 665-669.

A discussion of the role of school counselors is given by a practicing counselor.

"Outlook for the Counseling Specialties." Special issue of *Personnel and Guidance Journal* 52, no. 3 (1973): 139-183.

Ten different articles discuss issues and careers in counseling. Articles on career information for prospective counselors, the role of the community agency counselor, and the potential of elementary school counseling are especially relevant.

Stilwell, M. E., and Santoro, D. A. "A Training Model for the 1980s." *Personnel and Guidance Journal* 54, no. 6 (1974): 322-326.

These authors believe strongly in the need for counselors to be learning development consultants. They have proposed a systematic training model to meet this need.

Films*

Audiological Procedures with Pre-School Deaf Children (PSU) 1967. 30 minutes. #PCR-2165.

Preschool children participate in a program for hearing impaired children and their parents. Emphasis is upon audiological procedures, leading to differential diagnosis by extensive descriptions of each child's auditory status.

Audiovisual Supervisor (IFB) 1959. 19 minutes, color.

Objectives and responsibilities in this growing field of education are described.

Creating Instructional Materials (C/MHF) 1963. 15 minutes, color.

Contributions to student's learning experience through media are explored.

The Media Center in Action (CIF) 1972. 14 minutes, color.

Describes how visual images motivate the student, how the media specialist can assist teachers in use and selection of materials and equipment, the variety of audiovisual materials available, and how "open concept" teaching can extend the use of all media resources.

Public Relations of Testing (ETS) 1961. 11 minutes.

Importance of communicating the purposes and objectives of testing to teachers, students, parents, and the community is discussed.

Television Directing—Part I (IU) 1960. 30 minutes.

Includes undesirable and desirable pre-camera or rehearsal procedures and a look at the development of a program from its conception to camera time.

Television Directing—Part II (IU) 1960. 30 minutes.

This film is a continuation of discussion and demonstration of techniques and problems of directing, dealing with on-camera aspects of program directing.

Things to do

Volunteer or paid work. Seek out practical experience with young children. Participate in training programs and utilize professional advice and counsel.

Visit and observe professionals. Try to observe a specialist in action and understand the knowledge base and extensive preparation required.

Develop and exercise communication skills. Learn to write and speak clearly and accurately. Seek out opportunities for public speaking. Practice writing technical materials.

Read about jobs and interview people. Gather as much information as you can concerning the jobs in which you are interested.

People to talk with

Guidance counselor. A counselor can help you assess your career decision and plan a feasible course of action to prepare for and enter your chosen career.

People working as specialists. Find someone who *is* involved in a career you think you would like. Ask that person about their training, interests, and job satisfactions.

Parents and relatives. Your parents or other close relatives can often help you make realistic educational and financial plans for your career.

*Film distributors are coded and immediately follow the name of the film; see Appendix 1 for complete name and address of distributor.

5 Career Pattern Five

Provide to the General Public Goods and Services Affecting Children and Families

The key to careers in pattern five is the phrase "general public." Individuals who work in these careers serve the general public, not just individual children, families, or professionals. In serving the general public, such people provide goods and services that are particularly helpful to children, families, and professionals.

Most individuals in pattern five careers have strong knowledge and skills in the particular career area in which they work. Only secondarily do they acquire skill and knowledge relevant to young children and their families. Like professionals in careers described earlier, career pattern five individuals have the option of directing some of their efforts to areas that *will* affect children and families. Examples and descriptive information will be used to illustrate how each of these careers provides significant opportunities for improving the quality of life of young children and their families.

Typical decision survey responses for career pattern five

Because pattern five careers are so diverse, two types of responses have been included. Typical responses summarize and condense the main ideas and thoughts of all people who hold career pattern five jobs. Specific responses are those given by people in different careers. You will find it extremely helpful to review these responses to the Decision Survey before reading the interviews and descriptions of the careers in pattern five.

Step One: Why do you want to work with or for young children?

Question	Typical Response	Specific Response
1. Why do you feel early childhood is an important period of life?	*Young children require different equipment and services than adults. I think it is important to meet children's needs early in life to make sure they get a good start.*	*Children should be helped early to plan leisure activities.* *An early start on good nutrition will bring lifelong benefits.* *Beliefs about religion should be fostered in the early years to provide children with a firm moral base.*
2. Why do you want to take an active role in shaping young children's experiences?	*Everybody should be concerned about children. As parents, neighbors, friends, or relatives, we can all help make the early years of childhood pleasant and stimulating.*	*Television offers such a good opportunity to reach children. I want to help create educational programming.* *I want to be sure children have access to good books and information sources.*
3. What do you like about young children?	*Young children are vulnerable and require special care and concern.*	*Children are so curious to learn! It's a challenge to package information and products for them.* *The high level of physical activity, rapid advances in skill, and sheer enjoyment of activity make recreation work with young children very satisfying.*
4. What do you find challenging and stimulating about young children?	*Designing specialized equipment and services for children interests me. I find it challenging to try to tailor something to suit a child or to promote children through my efforts.*	*It's a challenge to design safe, appealing toys to help children grow.* *Children's questions often open whole new perspectives for me on nature and outdoor life.*

Question	Typical Response	Specific Response
5. What kinds of contact do you enjoy with children and adults?	*I enjoy children and appreciate their specialness as individuals. With adults, I enjoy conversation, exchange of ideas, and cooperative relationships.*	*I especially enjoy brainstorming sessions where a group of adults are thinking how to initiate a new product.*
		Informal chats and activities with children help me write appropriate scripts and keep a child's-eye perspective.
6. How do you communicate most comfortably and effectively with children and adults?	*I'm a talker. I can put people at ease quickly and share information readily. I get along with children and adults.*	*I think I do best when I'm demonstrating an activity.*
		I'm good at explaining ideas to children through pictures.
		I usually let children start talking and find I'm good at keeping things going smoothly.
7. When you work hard on something, how often or how quickly do you need to see results?	*I like to see immediate effects. If I don't, I am likely to work harder, work longer, or change my approach entirely.*	*I don't expect my work to result in immediate passage of a new law, but I like to think I have influenced people so that my work adds up to the achievement of some long-lasting goals.*
		Safety cannot come later. Now is when we have to have the necessary changes.
8. What kinds of help and support do you need to continue working on something over a period of time?	*I like to see that my work improves the quality of life for many children. I appreciate immediate rewards, but what counts most is long-term satisfaction with a job well done.*	*I can work for long periods of time toward abstract goals if I work with others who share my commitment.*
		Much of custody work, especially with very young children, is delicate. What counts most is the long-term prospects for the children in the arrangements.
9. What kind and how much responsibility are you comfortable in assuming?	*I hope to serve as many people as possible despite their differing needs. I am responsible for influencing large numbers of people.*	*While I work with different groups of children daily, I represent the museum and its programs and probably influence whether these children return.*
		Since I know my product lines well and know something about children, I don't hesitate to make recommendations.
10. To what extent are you confident about explaining the things you do to others who evaluate you?	*I am always open for suggestions from those who use my products or services. I can explain how my actions can or should impact on others.*	*I do extensive research and interviews for my articles, and while each represents my interpretation of events, I am confident about my judgments.*
		My decisions are reached after considerable deliberation and from a strong information base. I always try to give the reasoning behind my decisions and actions.

Career Pattern Five

Question	Typical Response	Specific Response
11. What sort of things that you do leave you with a good feeling about yourself?	*I feel good when I can help people get the product or services they want.*	*I feel good only when I think I have helped parents understand how to choose children's clothing that will be comfortable and long-wearing.* *I love to watch children on my playgrounds.* *There's nothing quite like receiving a positive letter from a consumer for a product I have been responsible for marketing.*
12. What kind of image do you want others to have of you?	*I want others to think of me as a person who exercises good judgment.*	*I would like others to see me as a person who has really good ideas and who works hard.* *I am creative, playful, and a grownup who takes children seriously.*

Step Two: What are your skills and abilities?

Question	Typical Response	
13. What is your educational background?	Grade School	
	High School	
	Associate Degree	X
	Specialized Training or Certificate	X
	Bachelor's Degree	X
	Master's Degree	X
	Doctorate	X
	Other	

Question	Typical Response	
14. What specific experiences have you had related to careers with young children?	Individuals in pattern five careers have experiences that are oriented toward dealing with the general public. Specialized training or interests will shape the particular ways they work. While all pattern five individuals display an interest in young children, not all have had direct experience working with them.	

Question	Typical Response	Specific Response
15. What general abilities have you demonstrated in your experiences with young children?	*I can observe children and remember the kinds of things they like and do.*	*I can plan activities and sequences of games that appeal to children.* *I have always been good at translating children's physical and mental capabilities into product designs.* *I seem to really have a feel for how children talk and what features of events are important to them.*

16. What abilities have you demonstrated in professional and social experiences with adults?	*I am friendly and easy to talk to; others seem to respond easily to me and respect my judgment.*	*I have always gotten along well with people, especially in group situations. I'm usually the one who starts the discussion.* *People are always telling me I am a good listener. I learned a long time ago that being a good listener is important.*
17. What abilities have you demonstrated in your experiences with groups and organizations?	*I can manage events and attend to small details. I can work with others or by myself.*	*I guess I have been a take-charge person ever since I had my first paper route at age 11.* *My colleagues tease me about all the lists I make, but I know that it is a good way to be sure I handle every detail on my projects.* *I am the sort of person who can keep lots of projects going at the same time. That is essential in my job as a legislative aide.*
18. What initiative abilities have you demonstrated?	*I don't mind being first or starting conversations and interactions with others. I am willing to follow an idea for a while to see what will happen.*	*Often I design 10 to 15 items for every one that ever ends up being tested by children in our pilot tests.* *I'll go out on a limb and see an idea through some rigorous market testing if I am convinced of its worth.* *I am a persistent person. I don't have much patience with people who give up at the first negative review they get.*

Step Three: What degree of involvement with children is best for you?

Career Pattern	Jobs
1	
2	
3	
4	

5. Jobs that provide to the general public goods and services affecting children and families.	Department store buyer, newspaper or magazine reporter or editor, dietitian, author of children's books, toy designer, recreation and parks leader, legislative aide, children's librarian, architect, museum docent, park guide, interior decorator, television programmer, freelance writer, radio commentator, religious education director, and many more.

Meet the legislative aide in state government

What background experiences influence a person's decision to become a legislative aide? What qualifications are needed to perform the tasks associated with this job? To answer these questions, we visited Janet who works as a legislative aide for the Child Development Committee within the office of the governor of a large, industrial northern state. We also interviewed some of Janet's colleagues.

Legislative aides may work as staff members at a number of different government agencies; some, like Janet, work for special committees, some work for program advisers, and others may work for senators or representatives. The primary role of legislative aides is to research, review, digest, and report to their office information pertinent to the issues. Aides follow legislation as it moves through the legislative process, updating reports and expanding informational summaries. At times aides may present their findings before hearing boards, committees, and subcommittees.

Janet's office is located in the state capitol in an area of government buildings, parking lots, and fast-food restaurants. She has a desk in a large open office that is also the workbase for the executive secretary of the Child Development Committee, his assistant, two secretaries, and three staff members from an office that directs projects funded through regional consortiums. Members of the Child Development Committee, a politically appointed professional advisory group, come to the office for their monthly meetings. The committee is broadly charged with overseeing, initiating, and advising those in government whose actions affect children. The committee wields considerable influence but has no power or authority to enforce action.

Janet works five days a week from eight to five; however, most evenings she leaves the office around six after a committee meeting. She works until her assignments are complete, regardless of how long a day is involved. We followed Janet around as she performed her job one day. Every day provides a different set of challenges, but a description of the series of events

The majority of Janet's information searches lead her to other legislative aides and staff members who work for legislators.

and responsibilities in one day will give you a general idea of what she does.

Janet arrived at the office to find a memo from the committee's executive secretary on her desk:

What is the status of H.B. 421? Prepare background information on this bill for distribution to the full Child Development Committee for their meeting on Thursday. Check with Representative John Dove, sponsor of the bill, to find out when the bill will be discussed in legislative committee meeting or brought to the floor of the House. Find out if he forsees any problems and from whom. As soon as you have this information, ask Ginny to schedule an appointment for us to review it together.

After skimming numerous telephone requests for information about Senate Bill 26 (Labor and Industry Standards for Food Preparation Areas), which bogged down in floor debate the day before, Janet drafted a message for the executive secretary outlining the floor debate, thus preparing him to answer the information requests. Janet had spent most of the previous day in the senate monitoring the floor debate because she knew members of the Child Development Committee were concerned with these standards that would ultimately affect all state licensed day care centers that prepare meals for children. Janet frequently must anticipate such concerns and plan her schedule so that she can readily provide information when others ask for it. After leaving word with the office secretaries about where she could be reached, Janet gathered her writing materials and left her office for the capitol building.

She stopped at the document printing office for the House of Representatives to pick up the most recent copies of H.B. 421. From there she went upstairs to the coffee shop to grab a cup of coffee and find a corner table where she could read the bill. After quickly skimming the bill to note any substantive changes from previous versions and finding none, Janet looked at the list of sponsors at the top of the first page. Some were familiar, and she knew through past experience that some sponsors had reasons for supporting the bill, reasons based on political ideologies, constituents' attitudes, and lobbyists' influences. Next, Janet thoroughly read every section of the bill noting any questions she had regarding terminology, finance, and content. She knows that the intent behind legislation is just as important as the actual wording. For example, one line read that the Office of Children would monitor *all programs for children.* Janet thought that this might later be narrowed to read that the Office of Children would monitor *all noneducational programs for children,* as the Department of Education would surely object to the present vague wording. Items like this are what Janet tries to clarify as she pursues her questions and gathers information.

Janet then went to the office of the prime sponsor of the bill to discuss the specifics of the bill with his administrative assistant. The majority of her information searches lead her to other legislative aides and staff members who work for legislators. There is a friendly camaraderie among all these people who depend on each other to provide much of the information they are collecting.

Before returning to the office, Janet made a trip across the capitol complex to the state library's document section to look up previous attempts to pass similar legislation. Sponsors and voting records on any previous roll calls are important. Information regarding the number of children to be affected, the number of programs operating in the state, and the number of people trained to provide programs had to be located to help establish objectively the scope of program need.

The Child Development Committee was on record publicly as supporting the proposed Office of Children, and Janet knew the committee would actively support the bill when it came before the committee of the House assigned to hear it. Eventual passage demanded that the pressure points of both the committee and the full House be anticipated. When a bill is read favorably out of committee, little time is left for intensive lobbying of the full House before the final vote. Janet was mulling over possible directions she might take in collecting more information when she glanced at her watch. It was past two, time for a late lunch while she waited for copies to be made of the documents she had requested.

Later, back at her office, Janet started files for the information she had collected. She usually keeps all the information related to one bill in a separate set of files, each carefully indexed. She often re-sorts and cleans files to keep her information up to date, fresh in her mind, and concisely summarized. Janet noted her contacts for the day on a running log, a systematic attempt to keep her sources clearly identified. She quickly sorted the phone messages into two piles, one to wait until tomorrow or until she had further information, the other to be returned immediately. Three phone calls later, Janet had agreed to brief a welfare department group on the status of Senate Bill 26 at their regular staff meeting; provided names for a senator's aide to gather statistics on child abuse; and accepted a dinner date that evening with a tax accountant she met last month during committee hearings. She laughed as she hung up, saying her social life was as impromptu as could be imagined. When the legislature is in session, the pace of work

Information regarding the number of children to be affected, the number of programs operating in the state, and the number of people trained to provide programs has to be located to help establish objectively the scope of program need.

for everyone is rapid, the hours long, and leisure time is often disguised work time.

It was five o'clock before Janet finished her phone calls, drafted several short letters for the secretary to type, gathered up her newsletter materials for work later on in the evening, and stuffed a week's collection of newspaper clippings in a file for quick perusal during breakfast.

Later in the week, after more research, Janet drafted a report on H.B. 421, discussed it with the executive secretary, and then produced a final version. She arranged several meetings for the two of them with the prime sponsor of the bill, with members of the finance committee who could provide insight into the funding mechanisms being proposed for the

Office of Children, and with other sponsors to discuss strategies for assisting the progress of the bill in committee.

Janet enjoys the interactions her job provides with many people who have numerous fields of expertise. However, there are anxious moments, for example, when standing in a huge government room reporting information or answering questions that committee members may have about legislation she has researched. The monthly newsletter that Janet edits for the Child Development Committee causes her moments of doubt and feelings of frustration as she tries to meet the printing deadlines. Often Janet must interview professionals across many departments of government that provide services to children and their families. She finds this stimulating, but somewhat outside the mainstream of her daily, immediate responsibilities.

Janet has completed her bachelor's and master's degrees in early childhood education, and feels they were necessary for her tasks as a legislative aide. Her past experiences in working directly with children included some precollege experience as a camp counselor and Sunday School teacher, and then student teaching in kindergarten and fourth grade. She had interviewed a state representative for a term paper in graduate school and sent him a copy. She received a nice letter the next month suggesting she apply for a position as a legislative aide to the Child Development Committee that was being formed by the new governor.

Janet is clearly effective in her job. The most important skill she has is a good background and competency in communication skills: reading, writing, and speaking. She is also a good listener, poised and able to maintain a hectic pace. She is analytical, both in dealing with information and in interacting with people. She anticipates accurately the kinds of information she will need in various situations and adjusts her interaction strategies according to the people she deals with. Increasingly she is learning to use the written word as still another tool, highlighting the nuances of the information she is presenting in ways that each audience will appreciate and remember.

Janet makes judgment decisions every time she chooses to include or exclude information from her reports.

Since she basically agrees with the aims and actions of the Child Development Committee, she said she has never had to resolve any personal moral dilemmas regarding the information she reports.

Janet considers her salary relatively low. Some aides are graduate students and receive credit toward their course work while serving a short time as aides. Others combine their duties with additional staff responsibilities during political campaigns.

Before leaving Janet, we asked her if she found many people in state government with similar interests, concerns, and training in early childhood education and child development. She replied, "Oh yes, that is one of the most rewarding aspects of working as a legislative aide to the Child Development Committee. Many of the members spontaneously share their information and skills with me. Many of the legislators I come in contact with are sensitive to the needs of children, willing to acquire more information, and supportive of programs that promise to improve the quality of life for all children. There is no question in my mind that what I do affects children, and that is a very satisfying feeling."

Meet the product representative for a children's furniture distributor

Fifteen years ago if anyone had told Gerri she would be a successful salesperson, she would have laughed and said, "No way." A friendly, outgoing woman, Gerri at forty-two is about to become a grandmother for the first time. Her husband Dan is a successful mechanic, who owns three repair shops and a parts and supply outlet. They have four children.

"Fifteen years ago," said Gerri, "I was up to my elbows in diapers, active in club work, and a trophy-winning bowler in a couples' league. The thought of ever working outside the house just didn't occur to me, but as my children entered school I found I had more and more time on my hands. After a few years of just moping around, I decided to do something about it. My decision to return to college wasn't easy. It involved a major change in the lives of all of us. By the time I graduated, I knew that my chances of getting a teaching job were slim. I wasn't mobile; I had to find a job in this area; and I was certain I only wanted to teach early primary. I applied to every school district within fifty miles, eventually had two interviews, but, in the end received no job offers. You can't imagine how deflated I was. Luckily, I was not too proud to try other things, so when a friend offered to help me contact a local company that was looking for a demonstrator, I gave it a chance."

The company distributes its own product line and those of several other small companies that specialize in children's furniture and related products. As a demonstrator, Gerri was responsible for making sure that all the salespeople knew how the products operated and what their best features were. She also supplied them with ideas to help convince shop-owners to stock new items. Gerri soon knew every item in the company's inventory and had good relations with the manufacturing representatives who placed their lines with her distributing company. When a salesman died unexpectedly, Gerri did not have to work too hard to convince her supervisor that she was just the person to fill in.

After two weeks on the road, Gerri was exhausted. Her territory was outside her county, and she made a major effort to be home every night. Gerri said, "It wasn't until this crisis point that I realized how much I wanted to work, how much I liked the sense of identity I got from working, and how much I cherished the independence of having my own paycheck! In the end we agreed on a compromise. Since it would be some time before I could expect a new and closer territory, I worked out a road schedule (three road days and two office days a week) that was suitable to my supervisor. I have been on that schedule for three years now and hope to move to a new territory closer to home by the end of this year."

Since Gerri alternates her road and office time, we cannot really outline a typical day for her, but we can give you descriptions of situations she is likely to deal with in both places. Gerri's office is piled high with manufacturers' catalogs and news releases announcing new products. She must keep herself up to date on price changes, product redesigns, deletions, and specifications. Cribs, playpens, feeding dishes, and strollers come in many different styles; she must know each for the current season. She must be prepared to pass on changes in price information to shopowners and to inform them of any recalls for safety reasons on items they have in stock. Processing orders consumes a major part of her time at the office.

Gerri works with little immediate supervision. She uses her time at the office to catch up on "road-news" from other salespeople, review ordering errors or difficulties with her supervisor, and return phone calls. Gerri works for a base salary plus a commission on all merchandise ordered through her. She finds the incentive pay of a commission stimulating, though she said, "I don't think I have ever consciously pushed an inferior product on a buyer just to get my commission. You cannot do that and expect your customers to respect your judgment later on."

Sometimes she really gets frustrated with all the paperwork involved in selling. However, she thinks the financial aspects of her job are at times the most mundane, the most important, and the most difficult. Prior to taking the job, she had no formal training in office work and finds that her general mathematical skills, constant organization, and attention to detail are sufficient to handle the tasks.

Gerri is busiest on the road during the two big seasons for her product lines. Prior to leaving for a road trip, she checks in at the stockroom and collects sample copies of catalogs, pieces of furniture and equipment, samples of materials, coverings, etc. She has her own car and keeps records of mileage, meals, and lodging for tax purposes. Her company reimburses her for all traveling expenses on a per diem basis, which does not always cover her actual expenses, hence the need for her own tax records.

Gerri covers a three-county territory that includes specialty shops and department stores featuring children's items. She tries to visit about 12 to 15 stores each trip. She always looks for other outlets that might stock her product lines and frequently visits potential buyers. She has increased the total number of customers from 20 to 40 over the last two years.

Let's observe a typical contact between Gerri and one of her customers. Gerri arrives at the store around ten in the morning when the manager and owner are not likely to be too involved with customers and have probably cleared up any snags in the day's operations. Gerri knows she will have only about 30 minutes of not-quite-undivided attention from this manager. He knows his needs, is prepared to order, and likes to feel he is choosing all his merchandise. Gerri left several new catalogs with him last month and expects that he will have selected some merchandise from them. Before leaving her car, she checks her files on the store, reviews the previous orders, glances at any notes she made during the last visit, and gathers up any material she may have promised.

Gerri has no appointment. She walks into the store and quickly locates the manager. A few friendly words and some well-placed questions concerning his perusal of the new catalogs gains Gerri entry into his office for serious business. The manager has decided to order some new items but wants to know Gerri's opinion of the sellability of a new feeding chair. Gerri calls his attention to similar items in stock at his store and asks which features seem to sell the best for him. He mentions that few parents seem to be buying the feeding tables. In fact, hadn't he reduced his order over the last year? Gerri looks the information up, knowing this was the case. She said later, "It is difficult to draw the line between giving product information and giving selling advice. I cannot make his business decisions for him. I would rather spend my time giving the most complete information I can about single products. I want to be sure the stores are stocking products that are appealing to parents and safe and durable for their children."

Briskly, the manager orders the items he wants. He asks a few questions about delivery dates from two manufacturers and notes he has not been pleased with their service. Gerri asks if he would like to switch to another manufacturer. Together they check product specifications for similar items; Gerri relates experiences of other stores with another manufacturer's shipping dates; and the manager decides to change his order.

Gerri notices that the manager is not as rushed as on some days and suggests they have a cup of coffee. She said she frequently has to take the initiative with simple social details that she feels would be second nature if a man were selling. Gerri shares the content of a recent *Consumer Reports* article on a child furniture product with the manager. By law such information cannot be used in promoting merchandise, but Gerri finds that many managers appreciate knowing what the ratings are since parents will often request certain items that have top ratings.

Gerri brings the conversation to a close with a suggestion that she examine the store's displays. She finds these informal tours helpful because she can often assess how much her competitors are selling to the store, and she can figure out what is selling fast by where items are placed.

We asked Gerri if she thought her knowledge of the development of children helped her in her job. "Why yes, I can help a manager interpret a manufacturer's suggestion that an item be used for three-year-olds, or I can help my customers appreciate design features of products that take into account developmental changes. For example, high chairs with safety straps are necessary for babies. However, a high chair will be useless as a child seat if the tray and tray hardware cannot be removed. I honestly think I bring a different kind of product sensitivity to my job. When I look at a product, I think of the children and parents who will use it and how well it will serve them."

Other visits on this trip include a stop at a large department store where the children's buyer has phoned in repeated questions about delivery of a

group of easels and sandboxes. Gerri dislikes handling complaints but realizes that it is better to face them and try to resolve them directly. Gerri finds that deliveries are running about two weeks behind schedule. The buyer is agitated, not just because deliveries are late but because some of the products were defective. When the buyer indicates an inclination not to order the merchandise again, Gerri suggests that perhaps she should cancel the automatic reorder that is used for such standard stock items. The buyer seems amazed that Gerri would do that. Gerri explains that the reorder has not left her desk, and a substitution is no problem. Faced with an alternative, the buyer agrees that two weeks is not a long delay and that the two defective items can be easily repaired in the store. The order is left standing, but Gerri has clearly made an impression for the future.

Not all visits are successful. One shopowner is not in the mood to discuss ordering, accepts the new catalogs, and says she will call Gerri next week if she wants anything. Gerri makes a written note to herself to followup. Having some unexpected time in her schedule, Gerri checks her watch and realizes it is too late to drive to the first store on her list for the next day. She decides to tour the business district to doublecheck if any new shops have opened. She stops briefly to chat with the young owners of a crafts outlet who were friendly and had once before steered her to a new business in the shopping mall ten miles away. She then heads back to her motel for a night of paperwork, a warm bath, and dinner.

Before we left Gerri we asked her what she thought she would be doing in ten years. "Obviously, my most immediate goal is to get the territory near my home. Sometimes when I daydream I think about becoming a supervisor or about starting my own furniture store. But you know, it doesn't matter how good a salesperson I am; if the products don't continue to be good, I cannot continue to be proud of my job. Sometimes I think I would like to work directly on design with a manufacturer. That's really an interesting question. I may think about that one for a long time."

Meet the director of a community recreation center

Eddie, the sweatsuit-clad director of the local community recreation program asked us to follow him around as he tried to catch up on his day's activities. "Housekeeping chores take a lot of my time," Eddie said. "I decided to do some of this routine stuff myself and use the money savings to hire more leaders for afternoon classes for kids." Eddie's housekeeping chores turned out to range from hauling out trampolines, setting up mats, checking lifesaving equipment around the pool, and filling the coke machines to typing out class lists, checking for phone messages from parents concerning their children, and salting the outside steps to break up the ice.

Eddie works different hours every day depending on the programs and activities that are scheduled for the building, a converted store in the middle of a downtown business area. Children can walk to the building from three schools, and public buses provide transportation for more distant children. Eddie's hours the day we visited were from ten in the morning until around ten in the evening when the girls' high school intramural basketball games would finish. Night activities are not always scheduled as late. Saturdays and Sundays are working days, though the evenings are usually free.

Eddie is in charge of operations in both outdoor and indoor recreational areas. He directs programs, personnel, maintenance, and neighborhood relations. He sets up schedules for game courts and playing fields, handles permits, assigns duties to staff members, oversees their work, and promotes future events. He enlists, trains, assigns, and supervises volunteers. Budgets, financial drives, and membership campaigns are also part of his job. "I deal with people all day, mostly adults who in turn run the programs and activities for the children. Occasionally, I drop in to see how things are going, but this job is pretty much like having a desk job without the desk."

Why had he decided to become a recreation director? He said, "In high school I was on the football team, and during the summer, members of the team often worked for the local day camp. We taught sports skills to the younger children, ran campouts, and served as counselors for small groups. When it came time to apply to colleges, I was thinking about working with sports or maybe doing some business administration work. The director of my home town program suggested that I apply to a nearby college that had an excellent program for training recreation and sports people.

"My job varies every day, and every season brings something different. We plan our programs to capitalize on the resources and needs of the community during every period of the year. Winter programs are mostly indoors except for figure skating and hockey. In the spring and summer we move outdoors to our forty-acre outdoor recreation area."

Eddie said he likes best the opportunities he has for increasing public awareness of recreational opportunities. "I like the chance to start early with children, helping them experience the joys of physical effort, team work, and self-satisfaction from doing something themselves. Along with my staff I can serve as a role model and show them that adults other than their parents can care for them and expect similar standards of performance."

Eddie feels that frustration on the job comes from lack of money, minimal community support, and low enrollments. "I can work really hard setting up programs, and then not have many kids enroll. I spend a lot of time talking with local businesspeople helping them understand how their support for programs for kids is really a good, effective way to support the community and enhance the quality of its life. I wish I had more practice influencing people. I am not the most polished public speaker, but I do reasonably well with slide presentations before Rotary, Lions' Clubs, and other groups."

Being a naturally friendly person, Eddie feels he has no trouble meeting and cooperating with others in the community who provide similar services. "Churches and school groups have been very open to new ideas, and we are able to coordinate programs to offer a broad range of activities to children," he explained.

We asked Eddie if he operated many programs for adults. "We have adult swim nights, a volleyball team, and some women's afternoon exercise classes. The thrust of my effort in the two years that I have been director here has been in providing programs for children and young adults. We even have an infants' swimming class now," he grinned.

"Unlike some other community centers which spread their resources to do a little of everything, I decided to focus my program's limited resources and try to do the best job I could for children and young adults. As I said before, I think serving children first results in the longest term payoff for later growth and community support for such programs."

The entire time we were talking with Eddie, we had been following him around the building, checking on various activities, and saying hello to children who called out greetings. Eddie stopped frequently to comment on an individual child's progress, noting for example that Sandy put her face under water for the first time and Tina was now able to float on her back. Eddie said, "Our swimming instructors are really top notch. Most of them got their early training here. It's great to see them helping others learn the same skills.

Eddie really cares about children. His interest in recreation and his job as a director enable him to reach a large number of children and to offer meaningful services to them. "I really cannot see myself doing any other job," said Eddie. "I may eventually move to another area, work in a larger or smaller center, maybe work in a big city or a regional unit, but really there is enough challenge, change, and stimulation in this kind of job that you could grow for a lifetime just trying to do it."

A check of the week's schedule of activities revealed that classes in hockey, skating, swimming, volleyball, basketball, gymnastics, and water polo, interwoven with discussion groups about getting along with yourself, getting a babysitting job, classes in makeup and poise, building a radio, reading for fun, woodworking, and needlepoint gifts, were but a sample of the programs currently offered.

We asked Eddie if there had been any major changes in the types of activities offered over the years. Eddie thought a moment and said, "No, I don't think a whole lot has changed. We teach soccer now, and perhaps ten years ago nobody wanted to learn it. We offer programs for very young children, tailored of course to their capabilities. You know, the biggest change is really not that noticeable from the list of programs offered. We have girls who want to learn hockey, who want to learn how to throw a baseball, and we teach them. Our girls' junior high school basketball team has always been around as an activity, but they win now because we support them more. I welcome the changes in attitude that have helped girls' sports, and I need to remember to do more to give active support to young girls during the years when they can most effectively acquire the needed skills."

Is there anything unpleasant about your job? Something you think a potential recreation director should know about before proceeding too far with career plans? "Any problems I have with the job are partly my own making, but I cannot help thinking that others must experience some similar difficulties. Sometimes I feel like I am married to this job. I do not have a wife or family, hardly time to date anyone, and I wonder what I would do if I did. Perhaps in order for me to manage my job and a family life I would have to work in a more stable program, one that did not require so much start-up work, or one that had more full-time professional staff to share the responsibilities.

"Frankly, the pay is not so good either. Since the program depends on community support for its existence, my salary must fit the operating budget. Hopefully I am growing more competent though and hence will be in a position to command more salary in the future.

"That's a pessimistic note to end on. Come on over here and join some relay races, guaranteed to shake the blahs out of anyone at three-thirty in the afternoon." Eddie hustled over to the waiting lines of children fresh from school, and called out times, pulled the gong, and yelled as loud as the children during the race. Later, he explained that his leaders were volunteers who had just started and were having a little trouble managing the children in the first few minutes of transition from school setting to recreation program. He said he often tried inconspicuously to demonstrate techniques and smooth over initial difficulties so that both leaders and children benefitted. "I'm not a talker," said Eddie. "I know the training theory, but I find that with the diverse group of leaders and volunteers that I have to work with, a little rubbing of elbows and side-by-side leadership right in the thick of things helps the most. That way, the leaders have self-confidence in themselves and often don't even realize the trouble they were headed for. I call it 'tuck-in' leadership support and training. I tuck it in when and where it is needed." That philosophy, we think, helps explain what makes Eddie run.

Look for these men and women at work in career pattern five

Recreation and parks: **Recreation director, recreation leader, camp counselor, park guide, community education director**

Careers in the field of recreation and parks are enjoying renewed interest and growth as Americans pursue leisure activities, and many communities strongly support parks and recreation programs and facilities. Increased demand for adult education courses has created still another growing area for directors and leaders.

Recreation leader. Recreation leaders work directly with groups to lead and organize both indoor and outdoor activities. They assist recreation directors by organizing recreational clubs, classes, and interest groups in playgrounds, recreation centers, youth organizations, child care centers, and other similar settings. Recreation leaders try to bring out the physical, social, mental, and creative potential of each individual. In doing this, they help participants learn healthy attitudes and fair play. Recreation leaders take care of equipment, supplies, and facilities; help train and supervise volunteers; and carry out other duties under the supervision of directors.

Recreation specialists organize, lead, or teach a particular group activity, usually at more than one facility or center. They conduct classes in a single skill, such as archery, dancing, puppetry, music, or gymnastics. They teach staff members and volunteers by helping them promote and conduct special skill activities. They must understand people's recreational needs and be able to encourage them to take part in group or personal activities. An even temper and an ability to influence people are valuable assets.

During the school year, recreation workers generally work 40 hours a week, afternoons, evenings, and usually weekends. In summer, they may work mornings, afternoons, or evenings. It is desirable for a recreation leader to be a college graduate with a major in recreation or a dual major such as physical education and recreation or business administration and recreation. Advancement is dependent upon experience. Employment competition is keen, but growth is expected in the field as a result of increased leisure time, higher incomes, improved transportation systems, earlier retirements, and federal grants for recreational programs.

Recreation leaders may choose to specialize their programs to fit the developmental and interest levels of young children. Many find that more advanced knowledge of physical growth and development is required to work with young children in tumbling, exercise, and sport skill areas. It is important to strengthen and promote growth, rather than hinder natural growth by forcing stressful activities and complicated skills too early.

Camp counselor. Camp counselors lead children and adults in recreational activities at day camps, residential camps, or resorts. They organize and lead groups in crafts, sports, nature lore, and other outdoor activities. Camp counselors safeguard the physical and mental health of campers, maintain discipline, and offer guidance. Thousands of high school and college students gain firsthand experience with young children in summer jobs as camp counselors. Camp organizations and resort programs need program planners who can schedule activities, coordinate staff and equipment, and handle many administrative duties.

Counselors are challenged by the temporary nature of their relationships with children. Short-term, intense relationships are the norm as children spend brief periods of time at camp or in resort settings. Counselors strive to help children build cooperative, supportive relationships with peers, learn skills, and relate easily to a variety of adults. Counselors can influence children's recreation habits and foster social skills as children interact with changing peer groups. Above all, counselors seek to help children enjoy the recreational and learning opportunities of a setting uniquely different from school and home.

Park guides. Recreation programs that operate on a daily "walk-in-basis" in city, state, and national parks require a slightly different type of programming suitable for a short-term visit. Park guides may work full or part time with schedules varying depending on the season of the year. During peak seasons such as spring and summer, park guides may work full days guiding visitors through exhibits, supervising exhibit areas, and performing numerous housekeeping chores. Off-season work may involve more limited contact with the public and opportunities to plan or repair exhibits, write information brochures on tours, and rearrange promotional materials on park facilities.

Training in science, nature, biology, zoology, etc., can be helpful in becoming a park guide. Many people are hired for these positions because they have had prior work experience with young children and/or the general public. Considerable training may be provided to acquaint guides with the features of the particular park in which they work. Guide jobs may be obtained through civil service exams or other governmental hiring procedures depending on the location and type of park.

Community education director. Adult education or high school extension courses traditionally have concentrated on basic and practical skills training, but they increasingly include more general courses for adults in the community. Courses on topics such as prenatal care, playing with your preschool child, and understanding children's fears are examples of the practical, informative, and often family-oriented courses available for interested community members. Carpentry, metal working, and similar trade courses can be used to construct items such as playground equipment while participants learn basic skills. Innovative, creative community education program directors can conscientiously orient program offerings to serve immediate and long-term needs of young children and families.

In many communities the director of community education has a full-time, salaried position connected with the local school system. The person filling this position often has graduate training in community work and training in educational administration and/or teaching. Directors must be able to work within the school system, effectively orchestrating the needs of the community program and the demands of the school system on facilities for regular programs. Often the director of community education is considered to have a public relations role for the school system with adult education offerings designed to attract and impress the community. As the general population of the country ages, present trends of more adults seeking education and information are expected to grow. Community education directors can look forward to expanding programs with growing numbers of students and diversity of course offerings.

***Business:* Buyer, salesperson, public relations director, store owner, toy designer, product representative (see interview)**

A number of careers in business affect young children and their families. Depending on their product lines, manufacturers, wholesalers, and retailers must at times be particularly aware of the needs and desires of this segment of the population.

Buyer. Buyers exercise considerable influence over purchasing trends in stores through their selection of merchandise from manufacturers. Regardless of how worthy an item may be, if buyers do not like it, chances are that it will not be available. Buyers can set a "tone" through the merchandise displayed in various departments. Selections of wooden toys, stuffed animals, and hand embroidered outfits will convey a very different message to a customer than an array of breathing, burping dollies; TV character toys; and plastic riding toys.

Buyers of toys, books, clothing, etc., seek to satisfy customers and make a profit for the store. In order to purchase the best selection of goods and learn about merchandise, buyers attend fashion and trade shows and visit manufacturers' showrooms. Before ordering a particular line, buyers study market research reports and analyze past sales records to determine what products are currently in demand. They

also confer with sales clerks whose daily contact with customers furnishes information about consumers. They check competitors' sales activities and watch general economic conditions to anticipate consumer buying patterns. Profit is important, but buyers are definitely in a position to choose items that meet standards of safety and quality construction.

Most retail stores prefer college or junior college graduates for buying positions. Courses in merchandising or marketing may help in getting a first job, but most employers accept graduates in any field of study and train them on the job. Many stores have formal training programs for all management and executive trainees, including buyers.

Competition is keen for jobs, and most of the positions are in metropolitan areas. Buyers often work over 40 hours a week because of sales conferences and travel.

Salesperson. A salesperson of toys, books, clothing, or baby equipment provides a necessary service to families. Even though contact with customers is a part of all sales jobs, the duties, skills, and responsibilities of salesworkers are as different as the merchandise they sell. The salesperson's primary job is to create an interest in the merchandise. He or she may answer questions about the condition of an article, demonstrate its use, and show various models and colors. In some stores, special knowledge or skills may be needed to sell the merchandise. In addition to selling, most

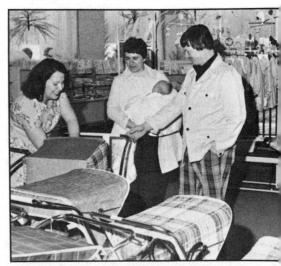

Responsible salespeople know the strengths and limits of the merchandise in stock and can communicate this information to buyers.

retail salespersons make out sales and charge slips, receive payments, and handle returns and exchanges of merchandise. In small stores they may help order merchandise, stock shelves, mark price tags, take inventory, and prepare displays.

As the contact person between customer and product, a salesperson has the most immediate opportunity to influence sales and selection of merchandise. Responsible salespeople know the strengths and limits of the merchandise in stock, can communicate this information to buyers, and will conscientiously call buyers' attention to similar products, pointing out the features of each.

Employers prefer high school graduates for sales jobs. A salesperson should enjoy working with people and have the tact to deal with different personalities. Other desirable characteristics are an interest in saleswork, a pleasant personality, a neat appearance, and the ability to communicate clearly.

Retail sales remains one of the few fields in which able employees may advance to executive jobs regardless of educational background. Job prospects are expected to be good because retail sales is a large occupation, and turnover is high. Salaries usually start at minimum wage, sometimes with a commission. Employees often receive a discount of merchandise. Salespeople usually work 5 days, 40 hours per week, which often includes weekends.

Public relations director. Moderate to large businesses frequently employ people expressly for the purpose of promoting their name and creating an image for the public. Public relations people use media and specially planned events to bring favorable customer attention to a business.

Large companies, prominent in the children's field, which manufacture clothing, furniture, food, and related items often distribute literature free to parents. Samples of products are provided along with written information related to child care and development.

As employees of a company, public relations people are first concerned with the promotion of a particular product or company image. Promotional materials can easily reach vast numbers of people, and with a reasonable balance of product promotion and accurate, well-presented supplemental

information, they can effectively communicate child development information to some people who might not otherwise receive it.

Many large stores operate public programming events that are intended to bring people to the store. Many stores now offer short seminars on topics such as child-proofing a home, dressing a child on a budget, or feeding infants and toddlers. Outside experts are hired to run these short sessions. Store public relations people work with buyers and salespeople to select topics and schedule sessions of interest to customers.

Public relations personnel must enjoy working with the public and must be able to coordinate a number of people, ideas, and programs simultaneously. They can provide useful information and services for young children and their families while meeting the goals of their jobs—the promotion of the business and its image.

Store owner. Setting up and running a small business is a complicated, though manageable, effort; some of the resources listed at the end of this section describe the details, especially the legal and financial aspects. Certain kinds of small businesses are particularly interesting to those who are exploring careers that can affect young children and their families. Children's clothing stores, toy, furniture, and children's bookstores, are a few examples.

Through their selection of merchandise, training of salespeople, and promotional and display techniques, store owners have an opportunity to serve

the public as well as earn a profit. Using a children's bookstore as an example, store owners can stock good, inexpensive, paperback children's books as well as hardcover books, thus promoting the use of books at home for all children and families regardless of income. Vigorous promotional campaigns at holiday time can result in increased business and, it is hoped, increased public awareness of the appropriateness of books as a gift for children of all ages. As active members in a local chamber of commerce or junior business club, shopowners can work to influence other merchants in the area regarding the need to provide high quality merchandise for children and their families.

Toy designer. Many toy designers work independently, bringing their ideas to large manufacturing companies and selling them as products. Increasingly, many toy designers now work in-house as part of a team charged with producing the next fast-selling doll or truck. Ideas for toys frequently come from television personalities and action programs, while advances in plastics and production techniques have greatly influenced the range of products that can be manufactured.

Toy designers are often not specifically trained in any design area, though most have drafting and illustration skills. Many spend considerable time observing children playing and talking to parents. Designers need to be knowledgeable regarding the physical capabilities of children at certain ages,

Children's clothing stores, toy, furniture, and children's bookstores are businesses which affect young children and their families.

knowing for example that requirements to turn knobs to open a box are unrealistic for a ten-month-old but an exciting challenge for a two-year-old.

Entry into design careers may come as a result of progression within a company's department, a lucky strike with a good idea, or from a design and art training program.

Specialized careers: Architect, interior designer, nutritionist or dietitian, children's librarian, lawyer or judge

Highly specialized training and technical expertise are required for each of the careers listed above that are characterized by strong professional identities and standards. Within each of these professions there are some who focus their efforts and specialize their knowledge to specifically affect young children and/or their families.

Architect. Architecture is a challenging profession both technically and creatively. The conceptualization of space, form, and function and the translation of these ideas into sound, constructible, and durable structures is the essence of architecture. However, few architects spend their days designing; much of the work is full of the detail of drafting, calculating stresses, figuring costs, selecting materials, overseeing construction and site developments, etc. Architects may work in firms headed by one or more designers, or they may work independently in small shops, perhaps specializing in certain types of structures.

Architecture offers numerous opportunities to affect the lives of children and their families, from mass-produced homes to custom-designed houses, public buildings, spaces, and working environments. Many architects specialize in the design of school buildings, day care centers, and institutions that will serve children. Considerations of scale, lighting, sound, heat, and color are thought to be different for children than adults. Buildings in which young children are expected to work, play, and thrive must be sympathetic environments for the demands and excesses to which young children will subject them. Architects must be knowledgeable about children's activities, developmental characteristics, and aesthetic preferences if spaces are to suit children. Designing schools and institutions for disabled children requires specialized knowledge. Items like ramps, special toilets and sinks, railings, and nonskid surfaces are but a few appropriate features.

Interior designer. Working through a store or independently, interior designers enjoy the pleasures of being surrounded by new ideas, colors, fabrics, woods, materials, etc. Specially trained to help with the selection and arrangement of a multitude of objects for indoor spaces, interior designers capitalize on their own design talents, aesthetic sense, and interpretation of customer preferences to effect various moods and schemes for living and learning spaces. Interior designers may specialize in children's spaces and needs. Knowledgeable about care requirements of various materials, sensitive to the preferences of both parent and child, and possessing a seemingly mystical combination of whimsy and practicality, designers for children's spaces often produce creations that particularly capture the personalities of their young clients.

Working with architects, interior designers often choose the color schemes, wall coverings, floor coverings, and design of interior furniture for schools, hospitals, and other public places designed for children's use. Knowledge of children's characteristics is a necessity since interior design choices must be both practical and appealing.

Nutritionist or dietitian. Nutritionists focus on the processes of food assimilation including the chemical properties of food and the digestive process. Nutritionists are often advocates of the importance of sound eating habits, the safeguarding of food processing, and the education of the public regarding the importance of good nutrition. Dietitians focus their efforts on the selection of food for meals and supervision of food preparation, tasks that require knowledge of body growth requirements for certain kinds and quantities of foods.

Nutritionists are found in a number of different settings in which their work affects young children. In academic and laboratory situations, nutritionists conduct basic research and disseminate information regarding the body's food needs and digestive processes. During periods of rapid growth such as early childhood, the body's needs are critical for later health. Nutritionists test foods and advise companies on nutritional aspects of their products. Nutritionists also work in government and in program monitoring or regulatory agencies overseeing the quality and composition of food products, providing nutritional advice disseminated under government auspices.

Dietitians may work directly for programs that serve young children, planning meals, supervising food preparation, regulating portions, and incorporating children's food preferences into dietary plans. Dietitians have special opportunities to work directly with young children and their families, promoting good nutrition through daily examples, recipe sharing in program newsletters, and demonstrations of healthful cooking techniques.

Children's librarian. Children's librarians may work in a public or a school library. Many public libraries have separate children's rooms or corners designated for children's books. The collections in these areas are often on lower shelves, with appropriate-sized tables, attractive reading corners, and bright, stimulating bulletin boards.

Most children's librarians work full time, usually serving as the sole staff person in the children's area. Volunteers, local college students, or paid library aides may help the librarian during peak periods of use. Some evening and weekend schedules are required of public library staff. School librarians work regular school hours. The employment outlook has been favorable.

Like all librarians, a children's librarian must be a graduate of an accredited school of library science. A bachelor's degree is necessary for admittance to any of these schools, and upon completion of training a master's degree is awarded. Included as part of a librarian's professional training are specialized courses in children's literature, display and management of story programs, and reading incentive programs. Many children's librarians have had experience working with children prior to or during their training.

The tasks of a children's librarian are varied, ranging from group work with children to paperwork. Generally the children's librarian is charged with responsibility for the children's area, the children's program, and the collection of books contained in that area. Physical arrangement of the space is important, and children's librarians spend a great deal of thought on arranging the books, tables, and equipment to attract and promote use of the books. Tasks such as cataloging and classifying books are daily necessities. Perusal of new books, ordering materials, films, records, etc., are all necessary ongoing activities.

Many children's librarians run extensive programs at the library including puppet hours on Saturdays, preschool story times during the week, and plays and informal dramatics for older children. Community outreach activities may include illustrated talks to parents' groups, visits to local schools, preschool programs, and day care centers. Children's film programs may also be managed by the children's librarian. In general, the children's librarian tries to

Lawyers and judges. The legal profession, including lawyers and family court judges, interprets and applies our highly complex legal system. In order to practice law in the courts of any state, a person must pass a written examination. The required college and law school work usually takes seven years of full-time study after high school. Almost all jurisdictions require that people appointed or elected to any court be graduates of accredited law schools and members of the bar.

Most lawyers are engaged in general practice and handle all kinds of legal work for clients. Their work with families may include divorce and custody hearings, representing juveniles in court, handling the legal aspects of

graduates has created keen competition for the available jobs. Prospects for establishing a new practice are best in small towns and expanding suburban areas. Salaries for judges vary greatly but are generally good.

Public service: Docent at museum, consumer advocate, lobbyist, legislative aide (see interview)

While there are many possible ways in which people employed in public service positions can affect children and their families, these examples serve to illustrate some visible emerging roles.

Docent at museum. By definition a docent is a guide, a trained member of the museum staff, whose duty it is to guide visitors through collections and exhibits, sharing with them helpful information and providing visitors with comments and critiques. Docents are frequently used to enhance specially mounted exhibitions and increase public educational opportunities.

Docents can specialize in certain areas within a museum, or they may handle all exhibits by acquiring specialized knowledge to complement the current exhibitions of the museum. Some docents regularly deal with children and conduct guided tours of special exhibits and collections to suit the expressed needs of children and parents. Docents are valuable resources in rooms where children can touch and feel exhibits, helping them fully explore the learning opportunities available.

Docents may be volunteers. Small museums may use a corps of interested local people who are willing to pursue the information and donate the time needed. Larger museums train and hire permanent staff. Docents may need some specialized content knowledge in the area in which they are to work in the museum, but for many positions involving young children, the basic requirement is experience with children.

Docents who work in children's exhibit areas, or who guide children's tours, need to have a firm knowledge of the level at which different ages of children can grasp information. For example, they know that with three- and four-year-olds the striking colors and shapes of Matisse's cut-outs are vividly exciting and cause for rapt attention, and for eight- and nine-year-olds appreciation of juxtaposition of forms and the simplicity of shapes is quite possibly as interesting as the color appeal of the cut-outs.

Children's librarians must have a gift for turning children on to books.

make books come alive for children and is constantly using a variety of techniques to accomplish that purpose.

Children's librarians help children select books, use the card catalog, and manage book borrowing procedures. Parents often depend on the librarian's advice in selecting and purchasing personal books for their children.

Probably one of the most important assets a children's librarian can have is a warm, receptive personality, a general demeanor and manner that invites children to question and helps them feel comfortable in a library. Children's librarians, naturally, must like children's literature, but beyond that, the effective children's librarian has a gift for turning children on to books.

adoption procedures, as well as generally advising parents and children of their legal rights and responsibilities. During a typical day a lawyer will meet with clients, research legal problems, and may appear in court.

Family court judges perform a wide variety of duties. They preside at trials, make decisions and judgments, and administer court operations. Their decisions on child abuse, custody hearings and divorce, and juveniles and delinquency directly affect families. In addition to courtroom work, judges must also research legal matters, study previous rulings, and keep informed about cases and legislation that will affect their decisions. A family court judge also needs extensive knowledge of available social services. A rapid increase in the number of law school

Consumer advocate. A consumer advocate has the interests and well-being of the product or service user as first priority. In recent years, many groups have actively represented the interests of the consumer, filling a gap that long existed in the chain of design, production, retailing, and use of goods and services. In the past there was generally no systematic way to funnel consumer complaints, concerns, and interests to responsible parties.

Consumer advocates serve a protection and prevention function. Some advocates work primarily on safety concerns and educate the public regarding the pros and cons of existing goods and services. Other consumer advocates choose to direct their efforts toward regulation and legislation to influence initial designs and plans for goods and services. Questions of toy safety, car seat usage for children, the effects of various food additives on children, and the materials used in children's garments are examples of areas in which consumer advocates have been active.

Consumer advocates can work for independent firms, supported by contributions of the public. Some advocates work within the government to monitor private industry. The title consumer advocate can refer to a particular sphere of responsibility within a government agency or private firm or may refer to a pervasive concern of an entire agency or group. Consumer advocates may work closely with lobbyists as they seek to disseminate information and more directly influence the legislative and regulatory workings of government for the consumer's benefit.

Opportunities to work as a consumer advocate are expanding, partly as public awareness of the need for such individuals increases and partly as people carve out career slots for themselves in these areas because of personal interest.

Lobbyist. A lobbyist is a registered supporter of a particular interest group or organization. Lobbyists are professional influencers, people who are skillful in convincing others of their view. Registered lobbyists draw salaries and publicly acknowledge the interests and powers that they represent. Lobbyists make it a point to follow the legislative processes and workings of agencies which have an interest in their sponsors. When bills, items of interest, or points of concern arise, lobbyists represent their sponsors by trying to influence the proceedings so that the sponsor's interests are protected and supported.

Lobbyists who represent groups organized for the purpose of representing children make it a point to be sure that children's causes are presented in reference to all pertinent legislative issues and agency activities.

Lobbying must take place in centers of power and decision making. State capitals and Washington, D.C., are places of high-level lobbying activity. People seeking to work as lobbyists need to have a good knowledge of the working of government, the mechanics of legislative proceedings, the points of possible influence, and the people to influence. Lobbying is a people-to-people activity dependent about equally on content expertise and personal initiative, performance, and persuasiveness.

Religion: Director of education, curriculum writer

Organized religions make special provisions for the teaching of their faith and the dissemination of church-related messages and materials. Terminology, titles, and duties will necessarily differ from faith to faith.

The local religious group. Terms like parish, congregation, flock, meeting, etc., identify the local branch of a faith. One or more individuals are often charged with specific responsibility for educational and activity programs for young people. The Sunday School director and youth group leader for example are often volunteer positions filled by adult members of the group. Larger local groups may hire a specially trained person and use a title such as education director or Christian youth director. This person may have received specialized training at seminary or theology school and has chosen to specialize in working with young people and adult education. An education director plans and supervises educational programs, being responsible for formal lessons, informal discussion/study groups, and literature describing upcoming religious events and celebrations. The education director may choose materials and supplies to be used in instruction, demonstrate and help train local volunteers in the use of these materials, and directly lead several educational groups. Often the education director may be involved in running a faith-related elementary school, preschool, or day care center. The education director will work in harmony and concert with the clergy assigned to the local group.

Regional groups. Individuals at this level may be charged with writing materials, visiting local groups, training local education leaders, and publicizing new materials and teaching techniques.

National groups. A national education office is usually responsible for writing and overseeing the production of lesson plans, study guides, activity suggestions, newsletters, and magazines that are part of the educational efforts of the denomination. Individuals with training in both educational and theological areas can be found in these positions.

Communications: Writers—feature story writer, freelance writer, children's book author; Publishing—editor, illustrator, photographer; Radio and Television—program specialist, commentator, scriptwriter.

All the media offer opportunities for careers that can influence young children and their families. At times during their activities these individuals may orient their work toward children and families, but few permanently specialize in children and family areas.

Writer. Professional writers write for money, whether they draw a regular salary or sell their work by the piece. They must know their subject, their audience, and be able to use language in a clear, effective manner. Reporters on newspapers often have journalism degrees and newspaper experience in high school and college publications. Feature story writers on newspapers are usually more experienced than staff writers and are assigned to cover news stories as they occur or are charged with finding material for feature stories. Editors respond to community interests, and feature stories may be prompted by requests for information. Feature story writers spend time investigating, interviewing, researching, and writing. Feature stories on choosing a nursery school, balancing a job and a family, nutrition for toddlers, and hospital stays for children are a few examples of the topics possible.

Similar to newspaper writers are writers who work for magazines or sell their work primarily to magazine outlets. Monthly columns in magazines on family and child-related topics are popular. Many feature writers specialize in certain fields, thus making use of their expanding professional and technical knowledge in that field as they research and write numerous articles.

Getting published is often a matter of persistence as much as effective writing and a well-chosen topic. Freelance writers send unsolicited manuscripts to editors and wait for acceptances or rejections. Freelance writing offers the challenge of sharing information while providing considerable flexibility in working hours with usually low or unsteady pay.

Getting published is often a matter of persistence as much as effective writing and a well-chosen topic.

Many children's book authors get their start through acceptance of unsolicited manuscripts. Large publishing houses regularly screen such submissions for promising books and ideas. Some children's book authors are also illustrators and may be hired to do illustrations, later expanding their work to writing as well. Persistence, ingenuity, and luck can combine to getting a start as the author of a children's

book. Children's books are a window on the world for young children, and authors have been notably successful in providing a wide range of opportunities for experiences through books.

Publishing. Many publishing houses have sections devoted to publishing children's material, books on family topics, public school and college texts, and professional books. Book editors do a variety of tasks in the acquisition and publication of books, from initial efforts to acquire titles and editing to working on final layout and promotion. Editors need a good feel for the market—what is needed and what sells. Almost all editorships and entry level jobs (clerks, copy editors, readers of unsolicited manuscripts) in publishing houses require a college degree and good command of writing skills. Specific editorial skills are learned on the job.

Illustrators or photographers produce the art work for children's books and other publications. Many illustrators have recognizable styles and over the years produce numerous books that bring to life particular characters, places, and scenes. Training in art is necessary for illustration work. Illustrators may work freelance or may be under contract to a publishing house. Besides the well-known illustrators, a number of career opportunities exist for illustrators to work in textbook and tradebook sections.

Radio and television. Broadcasting careers require varying combinations of technical skill in the use of equipment and media and personal abilities such as broadcasting, interviewing, voice quality, and personal appearance. Opportunities for careers in broadcasting are expanding as a result of increased public awareness of the effects of television on young children. Network stations are responding to concerns by increasing the number of programs aimed at children and editing other programs to eliminate violence and prejudice.

Directors of children's programs plan and supervise individual programs or a series of programs. They coordinate shows, select artists and studio personnel, schedule and conduct rehearsals, and direct the shows. Directors

may work under the supervision of a producer, who selects scripts, controls finances, and handles production. Many times these functions are combined. Both radio and television programs utilize similar personnel. A knowledge of children's interests and viewing/listening patterns is necessary.

Commentators on both radio and television may occupy permanent slots on a news or talk show. There are opportunities for these people to direct their efforts to items that might be of interest to children and their families. Occassionally special news programs for children are produced by local stations. Many local stations use a staff commentator to serve as moderator/producer of children's programs using local young talent.

Scriptwriters may work exclusively for one program, doing scripts for weekly shows or writing special event presentations. Scriptwriters working for children's shows must be able to meld content, language, and the special features of the broadcasting medium for effective results. Scriptwriters frequently work with professionals in early education or in particular content areas.

Many colleges and universities offer training programs in broadcasting, television production, and related areas. Graduates of these programs most often begin their careers working in small local stations and gradually move into larger operations.

Where do you stand?

As you have done with each previous career pattern, review your responses on the Decision Survey for completeness, then compare and rank your responses with those that are typical for this career pattern (pp. 55-58). Enter your ratings on the Rating Sheet. When you have completed the comparative rating for career pattern five, proceed to Part C (pp. 75-76) of this book for guidance in interpreting all your ratings.

Resources

Barry, J. M. *Opportunities in Journalism Careers.* New York: Vocational Guidance Manuals, 1967.
Deals with the newspaper industry, the rewards of a career in journalism, and the types of jobs that exist in journalism and related fields.

Breun, R. "Museums, Education, and Innovation." *School and Community* 62, no. 7 (1976): 14.
A brief description of museum education in Missouri.

Broderick, D. M. *An Introduction to Children's Work in Public Libraries.* New York: H. W. Wilson, 1965.
Provides a general knowledge of the philosophy and techniques of working with children in public libraries.

Bundy, M. L., and Whaley, R., eds. *The National Children's Directory.* College Park, Md.: Urban Information Interpreters, 1977.
Contains listings of local and national organizations focusing on needs of children and youth. Types of activities and publications are described with each listing.

Camp Counselors. Chicago: Science Research Associates, 1968.
Describes responsibilities, requirements, advancement, earnings, job opportunities, and outlook.

Career as a Librarian. Chicago: Institute for Research, 1968.
Explains what a librarian does, the necessary education, and the employment outlook.

Career as a Merchandise Buyer in Retailing. Chicago: Institute for Research, 1969.
Contains information on what a buyer does and the education that is required. Includes a list of colleges offering courses in retailing.

Careers in Law. Chicago: American Bar Association, 1968.
A discussion of the lawyer's role in society, legal and prelegal education.

Careers in Retailing. Columbus, Ohio: Ohio State Council of Retail Merchants, n.d.
Brief descriptions of over forty different careers in retailing.

Careers in Television. Washington, D.C.: National Association of Broadcasters, 1974.
Describes many aspects of the television industry and the types of jobs available.

Community/School: Sharing the Space and the Action. New York: Educational Facilities Laboratories, 1973.
A pictorial conceptualization of the variety of careers available in a community education setting.

Danilov, V. J. "Dusting Off Museums and Making Them Health Laboratories." *Today's Health* 54, no. 1 (1976): 34-39.
Describes the public health education efforts of a number of science museums.

Danilov, V. J. "Push a Button, Turn a Crank." *American Education* 10, no. 5 (1974): 16-21.
Describes a number of educational programs at applied science museums.

Educational Films: Writing, Directing, and Producing for Classroom, Television, and Industry. New York: Crown, 1965.
Explains aspects of filmmaking as well as the separate responsibilities of the writer, director, producer, and editor.

Greer, M. *Your Future in Interior Design,* rev. ed. New York: Richard Rosen Press, 1969.
Stresses the training and knowledge required for skill in interior design.

Groome, H. C., Jr. *Opportunities in Advertising.* Louisville, Ky.: Vocational Guidance Manuals, A Division of Data Courier, 1976.
Information on careers in television, radio, newspapers, magazines, and outdoor advertising. Also includes scope of the careers and background preparation necessary for various job options.

Hickey, H. W., and Van Voorhees, C. *The Role of the School in Community Education.* Midland, Mich.: Pendell Co., 1969.
Presents the philosophy, objectives, and activities of community schools.

Holland, J. L. *The Self Directed Search: A Guide to Educational and Vocational Planning.* The Occupations Finder series. Palo Alto, Calif.: Consulting Psychologists Press, 1974.
A retrieval system of information relating to 456 occupations common in the United States. The occupations are arranged in a system using code letters: R—Realistic Occupations; I—Investigative Occupations; A—Artistic Occupations; S—Social Occupations; E—Enterprising Occupations; and C—Conventional Occupations.

Hopke, W. E., ed. *Planning Your Career.* The Encyclopedia of Careers and Vocational Guidance, vol. 1. Chicago: J. G. Ferguson Publishing Co., 1975.
Designed to be used by those who want both general and specific career information and for educational planning. Gives detailed information and numerous photographs of persons working in the specific careers.

Interior Designer. Largo, Fla.: Careers, 1968.
This booklet describes duties, where employed, personal qualifications, training requirements, training opportunities, employment outlook, and related jobs.

Izard, A. R. "Children's Librarians." In *Children's Library Service: School or Public?* ed. J. G. Burke and G. R. Shields, Metuchen, N.J.: Scarecrow Press, 1974.
Discusses the work of children's librarians in public libraries and some of the problems they face.

Jackson, G. *Getting into Broadcasting Journalism: A Guide to Careers in Radio and T.V.* New York: Hawthorn Books, 1974.
Designed for the individual planning a career in radio or television news who wants to know exactly what goes on behind the scenes. Talents required, training programs, opportunities for females and minority group members, and unionization are discussed.

Judges. Chicago: Science Research Associates, 1967.
Describes the nature of the work training, qualifications, opportunities, and outlook for employment for judges.

Klever, A. *Women in Television.* Philadelphia: Westminster Press, 1975.
Contains interviews with 20 women in leading positions in the television industry. Of special interest are those women involved in the programming and production of children's television shows.

Lehmann, P. "Getting the Word from Consumers." *FDA Consumer* 10, no. 3 (1976): 9-13.
Describes the functions of consumer representatives who serve on over 30 FDA advisory panels and committees.

Meinhardt, C. *So You Want to Be an Architect.* New York: Harper & Row, 1969.
Stressing the complex training, this book describes the educational requirements, specialized jobs, types of architectural firms, and the apprenticeship required for licensing. Includes a list of accredited schools of architecture.

Myers, A. *Journalism: Careers for the 70's.* New York: Crowell-Collier Press, 1971.
Suited for the person considering a career in newspaper, radio, magazine, and/or public relations and industrial journalism. Descriptions and comments of persons in the various jobs makes this book interesting and informative.

Occupational Outlook Handbook. U.S. Bureau of Labor Statistics Bulletin #1875, 1976-77 edition.
Describes occupations and statistical data.

Occupations in Library Science. Washington, D.C.: U.S. Department of Labor, 1973.
Contains an overview of the field, occupational descriptions, and definitions of worker traits.

Recreation Director. Largo, Fla.: Careers, 1967.
Describes duties, working conditions, training requirements, lists of colleges offering major curriculum in recreation, personal qualifications, employment prospects, and earnings.

Recreation Leadership: What Is This Job and Career for Men and Women. Chicago: Institute for Research, 1971.
Describes the nationwide job opportunities with recreation departments.

Recreation Leader (Director). Moravia, N.Y.: Chronical Guidance Publications, 1976.
Describes the work performed by a recreation leader, the work conditions, personal qualifications and training requirements, and the employment outlook.

Recreation Workers. Chicago: Science Research Associates, 1968.
Describes the nature of work in youth-serving organizations, community recreation, armed services, and industrial recreation. It also includes requirements, salaries, and future outlook.

Reece, C. "Exploring Art and Science." *Children Today* 3, no. 4 (1974): 18-21, 36.
Describes the Smithsonian Institute's art and science programs for children.

Seay, M. *Community Education: A Developing Concept.* Midland, Mich.: Pendell Publishing Co., 1974.
Contains specific information on the staffing and administration of community schools.

Tebbel, J. *Opportunities in Journalism.* Louisville, Ky.: Vocational Guidance Manuals, A Division of Data Courier, 1977.
Describes an extensive array of career opportunities in journalism.

The Children's Librarian . . . Challenge to Creativity. Chicago: American Library Association, 1968.
A brief statement of requirements and training for children's librarians.

Totten, W. F. *The Power of Community Education.* Midland, Mich.: Pendell Publishing Co., 1970.
The theory and history of community education including components of a comprehensive program.

Whitt, R. L. *A Handbook for the Community Director.* Midland, Mich.: Pendell Publishing Co., 1971.
Provides a structure for the director of a community school to develop a variety of programs.

Wiggs, G. D., ed. *Marketing, Business, and Office Specialists.* Chicago: Ferguson Publishing Co., 1975.
A general reference for a variety of careers in business. Type of work performed, personal qualities, educational requirements, advancement, working conditions, and typical earnings and benefits are given for various careers.

Films*

Careers in Recreation (AI) 1962. 25 minutes, color.
Curriculum requirements and opportunities available for students of physical education and recreation are presented.

Children's Literature: A Library Liberates Learning (PSU) 1972. 30 minutes.
Introduction to the philosophy of one elementary school library, followed by a demonstration of the library in use is included. Examples of student interaction, a check-out system for the kindergarten, help of the teacher with selection of books by kindergarten students, available media, and library assignments of a fifth grade teacher are discussed.

Creating a Children's Book (ACI) 1971. 12 minutes, color.
"Jolly Roger" Bradfield, author and illustrator of popular children's books, tells a group of neighborhood children how he makes his books. Includes animated excerpts.

A Law Is Made (C/MHF) 1961. 29 minutes.
Animated chart explains steps through which a bill goes to become a law.

Maurice Sendak (WWS) 1965. 14 minutes, color.
This is a filmed visit to the artist's studio where he chronicles the development of his book *Where the Wild Things Are.*

*Film distributors are coded and immediately follow the name of the film; see Appendix 1 for complete name and address of distributor.

The Role of the Congressman (XEP) 1971.
22 minutes, color.

A description of selected roles of a congressman with a survey of many levels of interests and contacts.

Salesmanship: Career Opportunities (JF)
1967. 15 minutes, color.

The broad range of vocational opportunities, qualifications, techniques, training, sales tools, compensation methods in the sales field are presented.

Your Working Future: The Commercial Artist (EBEC) 1973.

This cassette and filmstrip provides an overview of career opportunities for the individual who has artistic skills and desires a career as a commercial artist.

Things to do

Volunteer or paid work. Seek out practical experience with the general public and young children.

Visit and observe. Try to observe someone at work in your chosen career.

Develop and practice specialized skills and knowledge. Seek out opportunities to acquire the specialized knowledge and experience necessary for your chosen career.

Read about jobs and interview people. Gather as much information as you can concerning the jobs in which you are interested.

People to talk with

Guidance counselor. A counselor can help you assess your career decision and plan a feasible course of action to prepare for and enter your chosen career.

People working with the general public. Find someone who *is* involved in a career you think you would like. Ask that person about their training, interests, and job satisfactions.

Parents and relatives. Your parents or other close relatives can often help you make realistic educational and financial plans for your career.

Information about careers in pattern five is also available by writing to the following organizations and requesting career information literature.

Advertising
The American Association of Advertising
Agencies
200 Park Avenue
New York, NY 10017

"Advertising . . . A Guide to Careers in Advertising"-55¢

Architect
The American Institute of Architects
1735 New York Avenue
Washington, DC 20006

"The New Architect"
"Getting into Architecture"-50¢

Artist
National Association of Art Schools
11250 Roger Bacon Drive, #5
Reston, VA 22090

"Careers in Art and a Guide to Art Studies"

The National Art Education Association
1916 Association Drive
Reston, VA 22091

"Careers in Art"

Broadcasting
Arco Publishing Company, Inc.
219 Park Avenue South
New York, NY 10003

"Your Future in Broadcasting"-$1.95

Business
National Business Education Association
1906 Association Avenue
Reston, VA 22091

"Careers in Business"

Small Business Administration
1441 L Street, N.W.
Washington, DC

Cartoonist
The Newspaper Comics Council, Inc.
260 Madison Avenue
New York, NY 10016

"A Career for You in Comics"-50¢ $4/doz.

"Comics in the Classroom"-50¢, $4/doz.

Clergy
Lutheran Church in America
2900 Queen Lane
Philadelphia, PA 19129

"Resources on Vocation and Church
Occupations"

National Council of Churches
Professional Church
Leadership
475 Riverside Drive
New York, NY 10027

"College Majors and Careers in the
Church"-20¢

Department Store Sales
Chronicle Guidance Publications,
Incorporated
Moravia, NY 13118

#375 "Department Store Occupations"-50¢

Editor
SRA-College Division
1540 Page Mill Road
Palo Alto, CA 94304

#245 "Magazine Editorial Workers"-55¢
#355 "Book Editors"-55¢

Government
Department of Health, Education and
Welfare
Social Security Administration
Baltimore, MD 21235

"Federal Jobs in Engineering, Physical
Sciences, and Related Professions"
OA-DP Pub. No. 018-74 (10-74)

J. Weston Walch, Publisher
321 Valley Street
Portland, ME 04104

"Careers with the Government"-$3.00

Manpower Administration
U.S. Department of Labor
Washington, DC 20213

"The Employment Service"

U.S. Department of the Interior
Office of the Secretary
Washington, DC 20240

"Careers in the National Park Service"

U.S. Civil Service Commission
Washington, DC 20415

"Federal Job Information Centers Directory"

Graphic Arts

Graphic Arts Technical Foundation
4615 Forbes Avenue
Pittsburgh, PA 15213

"Is Graphic Arts the Career for You?"
"Careers in Graphic Communications"

Interior Design

American Society of Interior Designers
730 Fifth Avenue
New York, NY 10019

"Interior Design Career Guide"-5¢

Journalism

American Council on Education for
    Journalism
School of Journalism
University of Missouri
Columbia, MO 65201

"Education for a Journalism Career"
"A Reporter Reports"

Book World Promotions
87 Chrislie Street
Newark, NJ 07105

"Do You Belong in Journalism?"

National Newspaper Association
491 National Press Building
Washington, DC 20045

"To a Rewarding Career in Journalism"
"A Career in Journalism"

Public Relations Society of America, Inc.
845 Third Avenue
New York, NY 10022

"Careers in Public Relations"

Lawyer

American Bar Association
Circulation Department 4043
1155 East 60th
Chicago, IL 60637

"Law as a Career"-40¢

U.S. Department of Justice
Washington, DC 20530

"Employment Opportunities"

Librarian

Office for Library Personnel Resources
American Library Association
50 E. Huron Street
Chicago, IL 60611

"Who in the World Wants to Be a Librarian"
    (6062-6)-20¢
"School Library Media Specialist" (6122-6)
"What's Happening to Jobs in the Library
    Field?"-10¢

Special Libraries Association
235 Park Avenue South
New York, NY 10003

"What Is a Special Librarian?"
"Special Library Careers"

Museums

Alumnae Advisory Center, Inc.
541 Madison Avenue
New York, NY 10022

#45"Museum Work"-50¢

Paralegal

The Paralegal Institute
3201 N. 16th St., Suite 11
Phoenix, AZ 85016

"The Lawyer's Assistant"

Publishing

ARCO Publishing Co., Inc.
219 Park Avenue South
New York, NY 10003

"Your Future in Publishing"-$1.95

Public Relations

Public Relations Society of America, Inc.
845 Third Avenue
New York, NY 10022

"Careers in Public Relations"

Quill and Scroll
University of Iowa
Iowa City, IA 52242

"Careers in Public Relations"-25¢

Recreation

The Institute for Research
610 S. Federal St., 7th Floor
Chicago, IL 60605

"Recreation Leadership—Opportunities
    Nationwide"

Religious Worker

Board of Higher Education and Ministry
P.O. Box 871
Nashville, TN 37202

"Vocation and Church Careers"
"Resources on Vocation and Church
    Careers"-$1.00

Division of Homeland Ministries
Christian Church
222 S. Downey Avenue
P.O. Box 1986
Indianapolis, IN 46206

"A Listing of Church Occupations"

National Jewish Welfare Board
15 E. 26th St.
New York, NY 10010

"Profession with a Purpose"

Professional Church Leadership
National Council of Churches
475 Riverside Drive
New York, NY 10027

"Listing of Church Occupations"
"Resources on Vocation and Church
    Careers"

The United Methodist Church
P.O. Box 871
Nashville, TN 37202

"Vocation and Church Careers Kit"-$1.00

Retailing

Committee on Careers in Retailing
National Retail Merchants Association
100 W. 31st Street
New York, NY 10018

"Careers in Retailing" (fact sheet 5)

Salesperson

U.S. Department of Labor
Bureau of Labor Statistics
Washington, DC 20202

"Occupational Outlook Brief—Sales
    Occupations"

Television

Television Information Office of the National
    Association of Broadcasters
745 Fifth Avenue
New York, NY 10022

"Careers in Television"-35¢

Writer

J. Weston Walch, Publisher
321 Valley St.
Portland, ME 04104

"Making a Living at Writing"-$3.50

C.

Evaluating your responses to help plan for your future

Please turn once again to your Decision Survey Rating Sheet. *Make sure you have:*

Completed the total ratings for each career pattern, and

Ranked each career pattern from 1 (most appealing) to 5 (least appealing).

You are now ready to evaluate your responses.

How to match your ratings

Look first at your total ratings. The highest possible total for each career pattern is 90, which means your responses closely matched the typical responses on each question. The lowest possible total, if no responses matched, is 18.

Based on these totals, you can now rank them according to how well your responses matched the typical responses. Use the following chart as a guide to selecting the appropriate letter rank for each career pattern. Record the letter rank for each of the five career patterns in the last column of the Decision Survey Rating Sheet.

You may have identified one or two career patterns for which you appear to be reasonably well matched. Is the career pattern you originally ranked number one a career pattern which you also ranked A? If your answer is yes, these are definitely the careers you should pursue. If the career patterns you ranked as two or three are the career pattern(s) on which you have obtained the highest total(s), then you should also explore them.

If your highest rankings of appeal of a career pattern are not similar to your rank for matching responses, you may want to go back to the Decision Survey and do Step Three again. At the time you first completed Step Three, you may not have been aware of many jobs and careers. If you still find you are not in close agreement on your ranking of the most appealing career pattern and your response matches, you may want to consult a counselor for further guidance, gain some work experience, or observe people in this pattern at work.

Perhaps you have not found a career pattern that is a good match for you. You may again rank careers in order of their appeal to you. If you still do not find you are well matched to any of these patterns, you may want to seek the help of a counselor in looking for careers that do not involve young children. Learning that you are not well suited for a career with young children early may save you from needless disappointment and difficulty.

Steps to take in planning for your future

Once you have identified a career pattern that seems to be a good match for you personally, you can begin to find out more about how to plan for the future. One of the important next steps is to **read about, look at closely,** and **try out** some aspects of the career that most interests you. The sources listed at the end of each chapter and those in Appendix 1 will help you do this. Read some of the books and articles suggested, talk to people in some of the careers that fall into the pattern, and visit these people at work. Ask them what they do and how they feel about it. Observe them at work.

You will also benefit from volunteer work in the types of careers you wish to pursue. Hospitals, schools, churches, and many other community organizations usually welcome people interested in serving children and families as volunteers. This will help you find out what work in that career is really like.

Some of the careers discussed in this book are usually pursued only after several years of **direct work experience** in the fields of early childhood education or child development. As either an unpaid volunteer or a regular staff member, you can make opportunities to learn as much as possible about children, families, and ways in which services are provided to them.

In some community colleges, career planning services are available to anyone in the community—not just the enrolled students—on the basis that any community member is a potential student. In larger cities, private firms are in the business of career counseling. Often fees for services at these centers are nominal, and the investment is well worth it in the long run if the service helps spotlight a career choice.

Additional training or education will probably be required for most careers described in this book. Once you are certain you wish to pursue a career, you will need to select the training program(s) that will best prepare you and which is economically feasible. Making such important decisions will require assistance from family members and others with whom you share responsibility. Guidance counselors can be of great assistance in choosing the right educational program for you and in

Evaluation	Suggested Letter Rank
Many of your responses matched those typical for people in this career. You will probably want to further explore careers in this pattern.	**A**
Some of your responses matched, while others were not at all similar. You may want to review these careers and talk with a counselor about whether they should be considered further.	**B**
Very few of your responses matched the typical responses. Unless you are strongly interested in these careers, you will probably not want to consider them. A guidance counselor could assist you.	**C**

Evaluating Your Responses

locating financial aid through scholarships, grants, or loans. Even while you are learning, you may wish to work part time or volunteer in a field closely related to that which you are studying. Close contact with your advisers and the career placement office will provide you with additional guidance as you pursue the career of your choice.

*****

The objective of this book is to help you identify a direction to take in selecting a career. You have explored alternatives and have probably identified a career pattern that appears to be a good match for you. However, you will continue to grow and develop and may very well have a different perspective on a career in a few years. Most people hold a number of different types of jobs in their lives as their interests and the job market change. No career decision is ever really final.

Appendix 1
Film
Distributors

AAHE—American Association of Higher Education
1 Dupont Circle
Washington, DC 20036
Attn. Ken C. Fisher

ACI—ACI Media, Inc.
35 W. 45th Street
New York, NY 10036

ADLBB—Anti-Defamation League of B'nai B'rith
315 Lexington Avenue
New York, NY 10016

AHEA—American Home Economics Association
2010 Massachusetts Avenue, N.W.
Washington, DC 20036

AI—Athletic Institute
705 Merchandise Mart
Chicago, IL 60654

CAF—Carousel Films, Inc.
1501 Broadway
New York, NY 10036

CIF—Coronet Instructional Films
65 E. South Water Street
Chicago, IL 60601

C/MHF—Contemporary/McGraw-Hill Films
Sales Service Department
1221 Avenue of the Americas
New York, NY 10020

COF—Counselor Films, Inc.
2100 Locust Street
Philadelphia, PA 19103

EBEC—Encyclopedia Britannica Educational Corporation
425 N. Michigan Avenue
Chicago, IL 60611

ETS—Educational Testing Service
Cooperative Test Division
20 Nassau Street
Princeton, NJ 08540

GA—Guidance Associates
Center for the Humanities
Holland Avenue
White Plains, NY 10603

HR—Harper & Row, Publishers
10 E. 53rd Street
New York, NY 10022

IFB—International Film Bureau
332 S. Michigan Avenue
Chicago, IL 60604

IU—Indiana University
Audiovisual Center
Bloomington, IN 47401

JF—J & F Productions
1401 Walnut Street
Suite 700
Philadelphia, PA 19102

MFF—Media Five Films
1011 N. Cole Avenue
Hollywood, CA 90038

NYU—New York University
26 Washington Place
New York, NY 10003

OSU—Ohio State University
Department of Photography and Cinema
156 W. 19th Street
Columbus, OH 44210

PC—Paramount Communications
5451 Marathon Street
Hollywood, CA 90038

Appendix 2
General Career Information

PDE—Pennsylvania Department of Education
  Box 911
  Harrisburg, PA 17126
  Attn. Ben Jenkins

PF—Polymorph Films, Inc.
  331 Newbury Street
  Boston, MA 02115

PMF—Parents' Magazine Films, Inc.
  52 Vanderbilt Avenue
  New York, NY 10017

PSU—Pennsylvania State University
  Department of Audiovisual Services
  Special Services Building
  University Park, PA 16802

TLMD—Time-Life Multimedia Division
  100 Eisenhower Drive
  Paramus, NJ 07652

UC—University of California
  Extension Media Center
  Berkeley, CA 94720

UEVA—Universal Education & Visual Arts
  100 Universal City Plaza
  Universal City, CA 91608

WWS—Weston Woods Studios
  Weston, CT 06883

XEP—Xerox Education Publications/Xerox Films
  245 Long Hill Road
  Middletown, CT 06457

Information about careers in all patterns described in this book is available from:

Chronicle Guidance Publications, Inc.
Moravia, NY 13118

The Institute for Research
610 S. Federal St., 7th Floor
Chicago, IL 60605

Richards Rosen Press, Inc.
29 E. 21st St.
New York, NY 10010

SRA—College Division
1540 Page Mill Rd.
Palo Alto, CA 94304

Selected NAEYC Publications

Order from NAEYC
>1834 Connecticut Avenue, N.W.
>Washington, DC 20009

For information about these and other NAEYC publications, write for a free publications brochure.
Please enclose full payment for orders under $10.00.
Add 10% handling charge to all orders.

How to Join

National Association for the Education of Young Children
1834 Connecticut Avenue, N W , Washington, D C 20009 (202) 232-8777

Over 31,000 parents and people engaged in the careers described in this book are members of NAEYC. Affiliated groups in over 200 communities provide opportunities for people who care about children to share their ideas and commitments. Each group provides a variety of services to its members, including membership in the national Association.

Membership benefits. Every member is entitled to these benefits: six issues of NAEYC's journal YOUNG CHILDREN, reduced NAEYC conference fees, voting privileges, and the opportunity to participate in several insurance plans. *Comprehensive members* also receive NAEYC's new books as they are published throughout the year.

For more information on NAEYC's affordable membership plans (including student membership) write to:

>NAEYC
>1834 Connecticut Ave., N.W.
>Washington, DC 20009

Index of Careers

Careers with Young Children:

Making Your Decision

Judith W. Seaver
Carol A. Cartwright
Cecelia B. Ward
C. Annette Heasley

Decision survey

for careers with or for young children

This survey is divided into three steps that will affect your career decision. Answer all questions in each step before proceeding to the next step. Use the section entitled "Surveying your interests in careers with or for young children" (p. 4) as a guide in defining terms and providing examples. Complete the entire Decision Survey before reading about career patterns one through five (pp. 10–74).

This Decision Survey and Rating Sheet accompany the book *Careers with Young Children: Making Your Decision* by Judith W. Seaver, Carol A. Cartwright, Cecelia B. Ward, and C. Annette Heasley. To order a copy of the book for help in completing and evaluating these forms, send $4.40 to NAEYC, 1834 Connecticut Avenue, N.W., Washington, DC 20009.

This Decision Survey and the accompanying Rating Sheet may be freely reproduced.

Step One: Why do you want to work with or for young children?

Question	Response
1. Why do you feel early childhood is an important period of life?	
2. Why do you want to take an active role in shaping young children's experiences?	
3. What do you like about young children?	
4. What do you find challenging or stimulating about young children?	

Question	Response
5. What kinds of contact do you enjoy with children and adults?	
6. How do you communicate most comfortably and effectively with children and adults?	
7. When you work hard on something, how often or how quickly do you need to see results?	
8. What kinds of help and support do you need to continue working on something over a period of time?	
9. What kind and how much responsibility are you comfortable in assuming?	
10. To what extent are you confident about explaining the things you do to others who evaluate you?	

Question	Response
11. What sort of things that you do leave you with a good feeling about yourself?	
12. What kind of image do you want others to have of you?	

Step Two: What are your skills and abilities?

13. What is your educational background?

Fill in the year in which you completed or anticipate completion of the following:

	Year Graduated	Year Anticipate Completing	Comments
Grade School			
High School			
Associate Degree			
Specialized Training or Certificate			
Bachelor's Degree			
Master's Degree			
Doctorate			

Other
    Describe:

Question	Response
14. What specific experiences have you had related to careers with young children? (Include experiences you have had with children and families, in organizing and supervising events, in disseminating advice and information, and in dealing with the general public. Both volunteer and paid employment are applicable. Be as specific as possible.)	
15. What general abilities have you demonstrated in your experiences with young children?	
16. What abilities have you demonstrated in professional and social experiences with adults?	
17. What abilities have you demonstrated with groups and organizations?	
18. What initiative abilities have you demonstrated?	

Step Three: What degree of involvement with children is best for you?

Directions: List jobs that you would consider as career choices for each pattern. When you have completed your listing, rank the career patterns in **order of appeal** to you (1 = most appealing to 5 = least appealing).

Career Pattern	Jobs	Rank of Appeal to Me
1. Jobs that involve working directly with children on a daily or very frequent basis.		
2. Jobs that serve families with young children directly.		
3. Jobs that involve directing and organizing programs and services for children and families.		
4. Jobs that involve providing information to professionals who work with children and families.		
5. Jobs that provide goods and services affecting children and families to the general public.		

When you have completed this survey, turn to Career Pattern One, p. 10.

Decision survey rating sheet

Directions:

1. Place your Decision Survey alongside the typical responses in the book and this Rating Sheet.
2. Evaluate the degree to which your responses match the typical responses for each question and career pattern.
3. Circle the number that best describes the extent to which your response matches the meaning of the typical response for each career pattern.

Key:
5 = excellent match
4 = good match
3 = reasonable match
2 = poor match
1 = no match

Question	Pattern One	Pattern Two	Pattern Three	Pattern Four	Pattern Five
1. Why do you feel early childhood is an important period of life?	5 4 3 2 1	5 4 3 2 1	5 4 3 2 1	5 4 3 2 1	5 4 3 2 1
2. Why do you want to take an active role in shaping young children's experiences?	5 4 3 2 1	5 4 3 2 1	5 4 3 2 1	5 4 3 2 1	5 4 3 2 1
3. What do you like about young children?	5 4 3 2 1	5 4 3 2 1	5 4 3 2 1	5 4 3 2 1	5 4 3 2 1
4. What do you find challenging or stimulating about young children?	5 4 3 2 1	5 4 3 2 1	5 4 3 2 1	5 4 3 2 1	5 4 3 2 1
5. What kinds of contact do you enjoy with children and adults?	5 4 3 2 1	5 4 3 2 1	5 4 3 2 1	5 4 3 2 1	5 4 3 2 1
6. How do you communicate most comfortably and effectively with children and adults?	5 4 3 2 1	5 4 3 2 1	5 4 3 2 1	5 4 3 2 1	5 4 3 2 1
7. When you work hard on something, how often or how quickly do you need to see results?	5 4 3 2 1	5 4 3 2 1	5 4 3 2 1	5 4 3 2 1	5 4 3 2 1
8. What kind of help and support do you need to continue working on something over a period of time?	5 4 3 2 1	5 4 3 2 1	5 4 3 2 1	5 4 3 2 1	5 4 3 2 1
9. What kind and how much responsibility are you comfortable in assuming?	5 4 3 2 1	5 4 3 2 1	5 4 3 2 1	5 4 3 2 1	5 4 3 2 1
10. To what extent are you confident about explaining the things you do to others?	5 4 3 2 1	5 4 3 2 1	5 4 3 2 1	5 4 3 2 1	5 4 3 2 1
11. What sort of things that you do leave you with a good feeling about yourself?	5 4 3 2 1	5 4 3 2 1	5 4 3 2 1	5 4 3 2 1	5 4 3 2 1

Question	Pattern One	Pattern Two	Pattern Three	Pattern Four	Pattern Five
12. What kind of image do you want others to have of you?	5 4 3 2 1	5 4 3 2 1	5 4 3 2 1	5 4 3 2 1	5 4 3 2 1
13. What is your educational background?	5 4 3 2 1	5 4 3 2 1	5 4 3 2 1	5 4 3 2 1	5 4 3 2 1
14. What specific experiences have you had related to careers with young children?	5 4 3 2 1	5 4 3 2 1	5 4 3 2 1	5 4 3 2 1	5 4 3 2 1
15. What general abilities have you demonstrated in your experiences with young children?	5 4 3 2 1	5 4 3 2 1	5 4 3 2 1	5 4 3 2 1	5 4 3 2 1
16. What activities have you demonstrated in professional and social experiences with adults?	5 4 3 2 1	5 4 3 2 1	5 4 3 2 1	5 4 3 2 1	5 4 3 2 1
17. What abilities have you demonstrated in your experiences with groups and organizations?	5 4 3 2 1	5 4 3 2 1	5 4 3 2 1	5 4 3 2 1	5 4 3 2 1
18. What initiative abilities have you demonstrated?	5 4 3 2 1	5 4 3 2 1	5 4 3 2 1	5 4 3 2 1	5 4 3 2 1
Total of ratings on Questions 1 through 18					
Your rank of appeal for each career pattern in Step Three of the Decision Survey (see p. 87)					
Your rank of response matches for each career pattern (see p. 76)					

When you have gone this far, turn to Part C (p. 76) of the book to help you evaluate your responses.

National Association for the Education of Young Children
1834 Connecticut Avenue, N.W., Washington, D.C. 20009   (202) 232-8777